EDUCATION
AND THE
SOCIAL ORDER

By the same Author

THE ANALYSIS OF MIND
Third Impression

INTRODUCTION TO MATHEMATICAL PHILOSOPHY
Second Impression

OUR KNOWLEDGE OF THE EXTERNAL WORLD
Second Edition

AN OUTLINE OF PHILOSOPHY

SCEPTICAL ESSAYS
Second Impression

THE SCIENTIFIC OUTLOOK

PRINCIPLES OF SOCIAL RECONSTRUCTION
Ninth Impression

ROADS TO FREEDOM
SOCIALISM, ANARCHISM, SYNDICALISM
Third Edition, Seventh Impression

JUSTICE IN WAR-TIME

FREE THOUGHT AND OFFICIAL PROPAGANDA

MARRIAGE AND MORALS
Fourth Impression

THE CONQUEST OF HAPPINESS
Fourth Impression

ON EDUCATION: ESPECIALLY IN EARLY CHILDHOOD
Third Impression

WITH DORA RUSSELL
THE PROSPECTS OF INDUSTRIAL CIVILIZATION
Third Impression

WITH SCOTT NEARING
BOLSHEVISM AND THE WEST

EDUCATION

AND THE

SOCIAL ORDER

by

BERTRAND RUSSELL

LONDON
GEORGE ALLEN & UNWIN LTD
MUSEUM STREET

FIRST PUBLISHED IN 1932

*The American edition appears under the title "Education and the
Modern World," with chapters II & III and IV & V run
together*

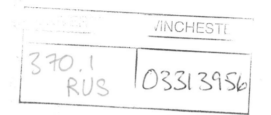

PRINTED IN GREAT BRITAIN BY
UNWIN BROTHERS LTD., WOKING

CONTENTS

Education and the Social Order

CHAPTER I

THE INDIVIDUAL VERSUS THE CITIZEN

THAT education is desirable is the opinion of all modern civilized States, but is, nevertheless, a proposition which has at all times been disputed by some men whose judgement commands respect. Those who oppose education do so on the ground that it cannot achieve its professed objects. Before we can adequately examine their opinion, we must, therefore, decide what it is that we should wish education to accomplish if possible: on this question there are as many divergent views as there are conceptions of human welfare. But there is one great temperamental cleavage which goes deeper than any of the other controversies, and that is the cleavage between those who consider education primarily in relation to the individual psyche, and those who consider it in relation to the community.

Assuming (as will be argued in the next chapter) that education should do something to afford a training and not merely to prevent impediments to growth, the question arises whether education should train good individuals or good citizens. It may be said, and it would be said by any person of

9

Hegelian tendencies, that there can be no antithesis between the good citizen and the good individual. The good individual is he who ministers to the good of the whole, and the good of the whole is a pattern made up of the goods of individuals. As an ultimate metaphysical truth I am not prepared either to combat or to support this thesis, but in practical daily life the education which results from regarding a child as an individual is very different from that which results from regarding him as a future citizen. The cultivation of the individual mind is not, on the face of it, the same thing as the production of a useful citizen. Goethe, for example, was a less useful citizen than James Watt, but as an individual must be reckoned superior. There is such a thing as the good of the individual as distinct from a little fraction of the good of the community. Different people have different conceptions of what constitutes the good of the individual, and I have no wish to argue with those who take a view different from my own. But whatever view may be taken, it is difficult to deny that the cultivation of the individual and the training of the citizen are different things.

What constitutes the good of the individual? I will try to give my own answer without in any way suggesting that others should agree with me.

First and foremost, the individual, like Leibniz's monads, should mirror the world. Why? I cannot say why, except that knowledge and comprehensiveness appear to me glorious attributes, in virtue of which I prefer Newton to an oyster. The man who holds concentrated and sparkling within his own mind, as within a *camera obscura*, the depths of space, the evolution of the sun and planets, the geological ages of the earth, and the brief history of humanity, appears to me to be doing what is distinctively human and what adds most to the diversified spectacle of nature. I would not abate this view even if it should prove, as much of modern physics seems to suggest, that the depths of space and the "dark backward and abysm of time" were only coefficients in the mathematician's equations. For in that case man becomes even more remarkable as the inventor of the starry heavens and the ages of cosmic antiquity: what he loses in knowledge he gains in imagination.

But while the cognitive part of man is the basis of his excellence, it is far from being the whole of it. It is not enough to mirror the world. It should be mirrored with emotion: a specific emotion appropriate to the object, and a general joy in the mere act of knowing. But knowing and feeling together are still not enough for the complete human being. In this world of flux men bear their part as causes of change, and in the consciousness of themselves as causes they exercise will and become aware of power. Knowledge, emotion, and power, all these should be widened to the utmost in seeking the perfection of the human being. Power, Wisdom, and Love, according to traditional theology, are the respective attributes of the Three Persons of the Trinity, and in this respect at any rate man made God in his own image.

In this we are thinking of man as an individual. We are considering him as he has been considered by Buddhists, Stoics, Christian saints, and all mystics. The elements of knowledge and emotion in the perfect individual as we have been portraying him are not essentially social. It is only through the will and through the exercise of power that the individual whom we have been imagining becomes an effective member of the community. And even so the only place which the will, as such, can give to a man is that of dictator. The will of the individual considered in isolation is the god-like will which says "let such things be." The attitude of the citizen is a very different one. He is aware that his will is not the only one in the world, and he is concerned, in one way or another, to bring harmony out of the conflicting wills that exist within his community. The individual as such is self-subsistent, while the citizen is essentially circumscribed by his neighbours. With the exception of Robinson Crusoe we are of course all in fact citizens, and education must take account of this fact. But it may be held that we shall ultimately be better citizens if we are first aware of all our potentialities as individuals before we descend to the compromises and practical acquiescences of the political life. The fundamental characteristic of the citizen is that he co-operates, in

12

intention if not in fact. Now the man who wishes to co-operate, unless he is one of exceptional powers, will look about for some ready-made purpose with which to co-operate. Only a man of very exceptional greatness can conceive in solitude a purpose in which it would be well for men to co-operate, and having conceived it can persuade men to follow him. There have been such men. Pythagoras thought it well to study geometry, for which every schoolboy to this day has reason to curse him. But this solitary and creative form of citizenship is rare, and is not likely to be produced by an education designed for the training of citizens. Citizens as conceived by governments are persons who admire the *status quo* and are prepared to exert themselves for its preservation. Oddly enough, while all governments aim at producing men of this type to the exclusion of all other types, their heroes in the past are of exactly the sort that they aim at preventing in the present. Americans admire George Washington and Jefferson, but imprison those who share their political opinions. The English admire Boadicea, whom they would treat exactly as the Romans did if she were to appear in modern India. All the Western nations admire Christ, who would certainly be suspect to Scotland Yard if He lived now, and would be refused American citizenship on account of His unwillingness to bear arms. This illustrates the ways in which citizenship as an ideal is inadequate, for as an ideal it involves an absence of creativeness, and

13

a willingness to acquiesce in the powers that be, whether oligarchic or democratic, which is contrary to what is characteristic of the greatest men, and tends, if over-emphasized, to prevent ordinary men from attaining the greatness of which they are capable.

I do not mean to be understood as an advocate of rebellion. Rebellion in itself is no better than acquiescence in itself, since it is equally determined by relation to what is outside ourselves rather than by a purely personal judgement of value. Whether rebellion is to be praised or deprecated depends upon that against which a person rebels, but there should be the possibility of rebellion on occasion, and not only a blind acquiescence produced by a rigid education in conformity. And (what is perhaps more important than either rebellion or acquiescence, there should be the capacity to strike out a wholly new line, as was done by Pythagoras when he invented the study of geometry.)

The issue between citizenship and individuality is important in education, in politics, in ethics, and in metaphysics. In education it has a comparatively simple practical aspect, which can be to some degree considered apart from the theoretical issue. (The education of the young of a whole community is an expensive business, which, in the main, is bound to fall to the lot of the State. The only other organization sufficiently interested in forming the minds of the young to have any really important share in education is the Church. The purpose of the State is, of course, to train citizens. For certain historical reasons, this purpose is as yet considerably mitigated by tradition. In the Middle Ages education meant the education of the priest. From the Renaissance until recent times it meant the education of a gentleman. Under the influence of snobbish democracy, it has come to mean an education which makes a man seem like a gentleman. Many things of little utility to the citizen as such are taught in schools, with a view to making the scholars genteel. Other elements in education remain from the ecclesiastical tradition of the Middle Ages, of which the purpose was to enable a man to apprehend the ways of God. Gentility and godliness are attributes of the individual rather than of the citizen. The Christian religion as a whole is a religion of the individual, owing to the fact that it arose among men destitute of political power. It is concerned primarily with the relation of the soul to God; and while it considers the relation of a man to his neighbour, it considers it as resulting from the man's own emotions, not from laws and social institutions.

The political element in Christianity, as it exists at the present day, came in with Constantine. Before his day it was the Christian's duty to disobey the State, while since his day it has, as a rule and in the main, been the Christian's duty to obey the State. The anarchic origin of Christianity has, however, left a leaven which has led, throughout its history, to revivals of the primitive attitude of disobedience. The Cathari, the Albigenses, the Spiritual Franciscans, all in their various ways rejected authority in favour of the inner light. Protestantism began in a revolt against authority, and has never found any logical justification for such exercise of theological jurisdiction as it has been inclined to claim after it had acquired control of the government. Consequently, Protestantism has been driven by an inner logic to the acceptance of religious toleration, a view which Catholicism has never adopted in theory, and has only accepted in practice for reasons of temporary convenience. In this, Catholicism represents the tradition of the Roman Emperor, while Protestantism has reverted to the individualism of the Apostles and the Early Fathers.

Religions may be divided into those that are political and those that concern the individual soul. Confucianism is a political religion: Confucius, as he wandered from court to court, became concerned essentially with the problem of government, and with the instilling of such virtues as to make good government easy. Buddhism, on the contrary, in spite of the fact that in its early days it was the religion of princes, is essentially non-political. I do not mean that it has always remained so. In Tibet it is as political as the papacy, and in Japan I have met high Buddhist dignitaries who reminded me of

English archdeacons. Nevertheless, the Buddhist, in his more religious moments, considers himself essentially as a solitary being. Islam, on the contrary, was from its very beginning a political religion. Mahomet made himself a ruler of men, and the caliphs who succeeded him remained so until the conclusion of the Great War. It is typical of the difference between Islam and Christianity that the caliph combined within himself both temporal and spiritual authority, which to a Mahometan are not distinct; whereas Christianity, by its non-political character, was led to create two rival politicians, namely, the Pope and the Emperor, of whom the former based his claims to temporal power upon the unimportance of secular rule. Communism, as it has developed in Russia, is a political religion analogous to Islam. It is, however, unavoidably influenced by Byzantine tradition; and there is a possibility that the Communist party may take the place of the Church, leaving the secular government to that degree of independence of ecclesiastical authority which it possessed before the Revolution. In this, as in other matters, Russia is divided between an Eastern and a Western mentality. In so far as Russia is Asiatic, the Communist party takes the place of the caliphate; while in so far as Russia is European, the Communist party takes the place of the Church.

The purpose of this bird's-eye view of the history of religions has been to suggest that the elements in current education which are concerned with indi-

B   17

vidual culture are, in the main, products of tradition, and are likely to be more and more replaced by education in citizenship. (Education in citizenship, if it is wise, can retain what was best in individual culture. But if it is in any way short-sighted, it will stunt the individual in order to make him a convenient tool of government. It is therefore important to realize the dangers inherent in the ideals of citizenship when narrowly conceived. Those who institute State systems of education will cause men to deteriorate, even as citizens, if they take a narrow view of what constitutes a good citizen. Only men of wide individual culture are capable of appreciating what individual culture has to contribute to citizenship. Unfortunately, in the present day, such men tend to be replaced more and more by men of executive ability, or by mere politicians who must be rewarded for their services.

(An education of which the purpose is to make good citizens has two very different forms, according as it is directed to the support or to the overthrow of the existing system. It might be supposed, in view of the importance of the State in education, that education would be almost always directed to the support of the *status quo*. This, however, is not the case. Except in Russia, the influence of religion and of the middle class is sufficiently strong to cause a very large part of education to remain reactionary wherever Socialists have acquired power. On the other hand, before the French Revolution, and again before the Russian Revolution, education, while not widespread, was in the main anti-governmental. In the more backward parts of the United States at the present day there is a similar tendency. State Universities tend to teach, more or less unintentionally, doctrines which are repugnant to the ignorant farmers who pay the taxes on which the Universities live. The farmers, not unnaturally, think that those who pay the piper should call the tune, but when they cannot understand the piper, or know what tune he is playing, they find this a little difficult. But in spite of these exceptions, education in the modern world tends to be a reactionary force, supporting the government when it is conservative, and opposing it when it is progressive. Unfortunately, also, the elements of good citizenship which are emphasized in schools and Universities are the worst elements and not the best. What is emphasized most of all is patriotism in a somewhat militant form: that is to say, a narrow devotion to the persons living in a certain area, as opposed to those living elsewhere, and willingness to further the interests of the persons in the chosen area by the use of military force. With regard to internal affairs, citizenship, as generally taught, perpetuates traditional injustices. The great majority of well-to-do young men, for example, felt patriotic during the General Strike when they acted as blacklegs. Hardly any of them had been so educated as to be able to conceive the case in favour of the strikers.

19

(Wherever an injustice exists, it is possible to invoke the ideal of legality and constitutionality in its support. Educators in every country except Russia tend to be constitutionally timid, and, either by their income or by their snobbery, to be adherents of the rich. On both grounds their teaching tends to over-emphasize the importance of the law and the constitution, although these give the past a para-lysing hold over the present. By reaction against this over-emphasis, those who desire any radical improvement in the world are compelled to be revolutionary, and the revolutionary's conception of duty to the community is liable to be just as narrow, and in the long run just as dangerous, as that of the advocate of law and order.)

There are, however, certain respects in which the advocate of change is likely to give better education than the advocate of the *status quo*. Animal habit is sufficient by itself to make a man like the old ways, just as it makes a horse like to turn down a road which it usually turns down.(None of the higher mental processes are required for conservatism. The advocate of change, on the contrary, must have a certain degree of imagination in order to be able to conceive of anything different from what exists. He must also have some power of judging the present from the standpoint of values, and, since he cannot well be unaware that the *status quo* has its advocates, he must realize that there are at least two views which are possible for a sane human being. Moreover, he is not obliged to close his sympathies against the victims of existing cruelties, or to invent elaborate reasons to prove that easily preventable sufferings ought not to be prevented. Both intelligence and sympathy, therefore, tend to be less repressed by an education hostile to the *status quo* than by one which is friendly to it.

To this, however, there are certain limitations. (Hostility to the *status quo* may be derived from either of two sources: it may spring from sympathy with the unfortunate or from hatred of the fortunate. If it springs from the latter, it involves just as much limitation of sympathy as is involved in conservatism. Many revolutionaries in their day-dreams are not so much concerned with the happiness that is to come to the common people as with the vengeance that they will be able to wreak upon the insolent holders of power from whom they are suffering in the present. On the intellectual side, again, there is a tendency for advocates of change to organize themselves into groups, welded together by a narrow orthodoxy, hating heresy, and viewing it as moral treachery in favour of prosperous sinners. Orthodoxy is the grave of intelligence, no matter what orthodoxy it may be. And in this respect the orthodoxy of the radical is no better than that of the reactionary.)

(One of the most important ways in which individual culture conflicts with the education of the citizen, narrowly conceived, is in respect of the

21

scientific attitude towards doubtful questions. Science has developed a certain technique, which is essentially a technique of discovery, that is to say, of change. The scientific frame of mind is, broadly speaking, that which facilitates discovery, not that which causes a man to have an unwavering belief in the present tenets of science. A well-educated citizen is likely to be incapable of discovery, since he will respect his elders and betters, reverence the great men of the past generation, and look with horror upon all subversive doctrines. The modern State, which is built upon science, is therefore in a difficulty. Some States prefer unorthodox people who invent new explosives, others prefer that their young men should be orthodox, and should carry on the great traditions of the past. The Byzantines, when they could have purchased the help of the West by a few theological concessions, chose instead to preserve their orthodoxy, and suffered defeat at the hands of the Turk. Similarly, the British Admiralty, when faced with the terrible alternative of either listening to subversive young men or becoming obsolete through admiration of Nelson, prefers the latter alternative, whatever sufferings may be entailed by its reverence for the great traditions of our ancestors. So at least it is said by those who should know.

It is one of the contradictions of our time that science, which is the source of power, and more particularly of governmental power, depends for

its advancement upon an essentially anarchic state
of mind in the investigator. The scientific state of
mind is neither sceptical nor dogmatic. The sceptic
holds that the truth is undiscoverable, while the
dogmatist holds that it is already discovered. The
man of science holds that the truth is discoverable
though not discovered, at any rate in the matters
which he is investigating. But even to say that the
truth is discoverable is to say rather more than the
genuine man of science believes, since he does not
conceive his discoveries as final and absolute, but
as approximations subject to future correction.
Absence of finality is of the essence of the scientific
spirit. The beliefs of the man of science are therefore tentative and undogmatic. But in so far as
they result from his own researches, they are personal, not social. They depend, that is to say, upon
what he himself has ascertained by observation
and inference, not upon what society considers it
prudent for the good citizen to believe. This conflict between the scientific spirit and the governmental use of science is likely ultimately to bring
scientific progress to a standstill, since scientific
technique will be increasingly used to instil orthodoxy and credulity. If this is not to happen, it will
be necessary that boys showing a certain degree of
aptitude for science shall be exempted from the
usual training in citizenship, and given a licence to
think. Persons reaching a certain level in examinations will be allowed to place after their names the

letters L.T., meaning "Licensed to Think." Such persons shall thereafter never be disqualified from any post on the ground that they think their superiors fools.)

Speaking more seriously,(the whole conception of truth is one which is difficult to reconcile with the usual ideals of citizenship. It may, of course, be said, as is said by pragmatists, that the conception of truth in its traditional form has no validity, and that the truth is only what it is convenient to believe. If this be the case, truth can be determined by Act of Parliament. Leigh Hunt found it to be inconvenient to believe that the Prince Regent was fat, since this opinion caused him to be incarcerated. It follows that the Prince Regent was thin. It is difficult in such a case as this to accept the pragmatist's philosophy. One can hardly resist the conviction that there is something objectively and absolutely true about the proposition that the Prince Regent was fat. I can, of course, imagine a large number of arguments designed to escape from this conclusion. The word "fat" is a relative term. I remember that when the late Master of Christ's, by no means a small man, found himself at dinner between two of the most eminent writers of our time, he remarked that he was having the unusual experience of feeling thin. Compared to some prize pigs the Prince Regent may have been thin. Therefore, in order to make Leigh Hunt's statement accurate, it would be necessary to say that the Prince Regent belonged to the fattest one per cent. of adult males, or some such statement as that. It would be possible to say: "the ratio of the Prince Regent's weight to His Highness's height exceeds that of all but one per cent. of His Majesty's adult male subjects." This statement might, of course, be on the margin of doubt, but if so it could be made quite certainly correct by substituting two per cent. for one per cent. It cannot be seriously maintained that such a proposition is true because it is convenient to believe it, or becomes false through the fact that it is criminal to utter it. I have chosen an instance from a time more than a hundred years since, and one which no longer arouses political passion. But analogous matters of fact are at the present day of interest to governments, and there are still many propositions which no person of scientific mind can deny, but which no person who wishes to keep out of jail will utter. All the governments of the world adopt elaborate methods of concealing truths which they consider undesirable, and inflict various forms of penalty upon those who spread knowledge which is thought bad for the population. This applies especially to knowledge of the kind which is considered seditious, and the kind which is considered obscene. I shall not give instances, since, if I did, I should myself fall under the ban of the law.

For the reasons which we have been considering, education in citizenship has grave dangers. Nevertheless, the argument in favour of some

25

education designed to produce social cohesion is overwhelming.

(The amenities of civilized life depend upon co-operation, and every increase in industrialism demands an increase in co-operation.) China, for example, has all the requisites for prosperity and high culture, except the existence of a strong centralized government. Latin America, ever since it emancipated itself from Spain and Portugal, has been kept backward by the anarchic tendencies of its inhabitants. There is some evidence that the United States is preparing to follow the example of Latin America. Certainly the greatest danger from which the United States suffers at the present time is the absence of any vivid sense of citizenship on the part of a large proportion of its inhabitants. This cannot be attributed to any failure to emphasize citizenship in education; on the contrary, the whole educational machine in America, from the public schools to the Universities, is concerned to emphasize citizenship, and to impress its duties upon the youthful mind. In spite of this educational effort, the average American, owing either to the pioneering tradition or to the fact that his recent ancestors were Europeans, does not have that instinctive sense of the community which exists in the older countries of Europe. And unless he acquires it there, is a danger that the whole industrial system may break down.

(Apart from national cohesion within the State,

which is all that State education attempts to achieve at present, international cohesion, and a sense of the whole human race as one co-operative unit, is becoming increasingly necessary if our scientific civilization is to survive. I think this survival will demand, as a minimum condition, the establishment of a world State and the subsequent institution of a world-wide system of education designed to produce loyalty to the world State. No doubt such a system of education will entail, at any rate for a century or two, certain crudities which will militate against the development of the individual. But if the alternative is chaos and the death of civilization, the price will be worth paying. Modern communities are more closely knit than those of past times in their economic and political structure; and if they are to be successful there must be a corresponding increase in the sense of citizenship on the part of individual men and women. Loyalty to a world State would not, of course, entail the worst feature of loyalty to one of the existing States, namely, the encouragement of war. But it might entail considerable curtailment of the intellectual and of the æsthetic impulses. I think, nevertheless, that the most vital need of the near future will be the cultivation of a vivid sense of citizenship of the world. When once the world as a single economic and political unit has become secure, it will be possible for individual culture to revive. But until that time our whole civilization remains in jeopardy. Considered *sub*

27

specie aeternitatis, the education of the individual is to my mind a finer thing than the education of the citizen; but considered politically, in relation to the needs of the time, the education of the citizen must, I fear, take the first place.)

CHAPTER II

THE NEGATIVE THEORY OF EDUCATION

THREE divergent theories of education all have their advocates in the present day. (Of these the first considers that the sole purpose of education is to provide opportunities of growth and to remove hampering influences. The second holds that the purpose of education is to give culture to the individual and to develop his capacities to the utmost. The third holds that education is to be considered rather in relation to the community than in relation to the individual, and that its business is to train useful citizens. Of these theories the first is the newest while the third is the oldest. The second and third theories, which we considered in the preceding chapter, have in common the view that education can give something positive, while the first regards its function as purely negative. No actual education proceeds wholly and completely on any one of the three theories. All three in varying proportions are found in every system that actually exists. It is, I think, fairly clear that no one of the three is adequate by itself, and that the choice of a right system of education depends in great measure upon the adoption of a due proportion between the three theories. For my part, while I think that there is more truth in the first theory, which we may call the negative view of education, I do not think that it contains by any means the whole truth. The negative view has dominated much progressive thinking on education. It is part of the general creed of liberty which has inspired liberal thought since the time of Rousseau. Oddly enough, political liberalism has been connected with the belief in compulsory education, while the belief in freedom in education exists in great measure among Socialists, and even Communists. Nevertheless, this belief is ideologically connected with liberalism, and has the same degree of truth and falsehood that belongs to the conception of liberty in other spheres.

Until very recent times hardly anybody questioned the view that it is the business of education to train the child in the way he should go. He was to be taught moral maxims, habits of industry, and a stock of knowledge proportional to his social station. The methods by which this was to be achieved were rough and ready, in fact not unlike those employed in the training of horses. What the whip was to do to the horse the rod was to do to the child. It cannot be denied that this system, for all its crudity, produced on the whole the results at which it aimed. It was only a minority that suffered education, but in that minority certain habits had been formed—habits of self-discipline and social conformity, of capacity for command, and of harshness that took no account of human needs. Men trained under Dr. Keate and similar pedagogues made our England what it is, and extended the blessings of our civilization to the benighted heathen in India and Africa. I do not wish to belittle this achievement, and I am not sure that it would have been possible by any other method with the same economy of effort. Its products, owing to a certain Spartan toughness and to a complete incapacity for intellectual doubt, acquired the qualities needed by an imperial race among backward peoples. They were able to pass on the stern rule to which they had been subjected in youth, and to avoid the realization that what they supposed to be their education had starved the intelligence and the emotions in order to strengthen the will. In America a similar result was achieved by Puritanism while it remained vigorous.

The Romantic Movement was essentially a protest in the name of the emotions against the previous undue emphasis upon the will. The Romantic Movement achieved something as regards the treatment of very young children, but in the main the educational authorities were too firmly entrenched and too much habituated to command to be appreciably affected by the softer ideals of the Romantics. It is only in our own day that their general outlook upon life has begun to produce any really widespread effect upon educational theory, but just as *laisser faire* in economics has had to give way to new forms of ordered planning, so in education *laisser faire*, while it is a necessary stage, is not, I think, the last word. I propose in this chapter to state the case in its favour, and then to examine its limitations.

The case for the greatest possible freedom in education is a very strong one. To begin with, absence of freedom involves conflicts with adults, which frequently have a much more profound psychological effect than was realized until very recently. The child who is in any way coerced tends to respond with hatred, and if, as is usual, he is not able to give free vent to his hatred, it festers inwardly, and may sink into the unconscious with all kinds of strange consequences throughout the rest of life. The father as the object of hatred may come to be replaced by the State, the Church, or a foreign nation, thus leading a man to become an anarchist, an atheist, or a militarist as the case may be. Or again, hatred of the authorities who oppress the child may become transferred into a desire to inflict equal oppression later on upon the next generation. Or there may be merely a general moroseness, making pleasant social and personal relations impossible. I found one day in school a boy of medium size ill-treating a smaller boy. I expostulated, but he replied: "The bigs hit me, so I hit the babies; that's fair." In these words he epitomized the history of the human race.

Another effect of compulsion in education is that it destroys originality and intellectual interest. Desire for knowledge, at any rate for a good deal of know-

32

ledge, is natural to the young, but is generally destroyed by the fact that they are given more than they desire or can assimilate. Children who are forced to eat acquire a loathing for food, and children who are forced to learn acquire a loathing for knowledge. When they think, they do not think spontaneously in the way in which they run or jump or shout: they think with a view to pleasing some adult, and therefore with an attempt at correctness rather than from natural curiosity. The killing of spontaneity is especially disastrous in artistic directions. Children who are taught literature or painting or music to excess, or with a view to correctness rather than to self-expression, become progressively less interested in the aesthetic side of life. Even a boy's interest in mechanical devices can be killed by too much instruction. If you teach a boy the principle of the common pump in lesson-time, he will try to avoid acquiring the knowledge you are trying to impart, whereas if you have a pump in your back yard and forbid him to touch it he will spend all his leisure studying it. A great many of these troubles are avoided by making lessons voluntary. There is no longer friction between teacher and pupil, and in a fairly large proportion of cases the pupils consider the knowledge imparted by the teacher worth having. Their initiative is not destroyed, because it is by their own choice that they learn, and they do not accumulate masses of undigested hate to lie festering in the

a 33

unconscious throughout the rest of life. The arguments for free speech, for freedom from politeness, and for freedom in regard to sex knowledge are even stronger, but I shall consider these matters separately at a later stage.

For all these reasons, reforming educators tend, and I think tend rightly, towards greater and greater freedom in the school. I do not think, however, that freedom in school can be erected into an absolute principle. It has its limitations, and it is important to realize what they are.

As one of the most obvious examples we may take cleanliness. I should like to say to begin with that most children of well-to-do parents are kept a great deal too clean. Parents excuse their behaviour on the ground that cleanliness is hygienic, but the motive for making it excessive is one of snobbery. If you see two children, one of whom is clean and the other is dirty, you tend to suppose that the clean one's parents have a larger income than the parents of the dirty one. Consequently snobs try to keep their children very clean. This is an abominable tyranny which interferes with the children doing a great many of the things they had better be doing. From the point of view of health it is well that the children should be clean twice a day, when they get up in the morning and when they go to bed at night. Between these two painful moments they should be grubbing about exploring the world, especially its grimier portions, ruining their clothes

34

and wiping muddy hands on their faces. To deprive children of these pleasures is to lessen their initiative, their impulse towards exploration, and their acquisition of useful muscular habits. But although dirt is such an admirable thing, cleanliness also has its place in the morning and evening, as we said before, and even this limited place it will not secure in a child's life except through a good deal of coercion. If we wore no clothes and lived in a hot climate, we should get all the cleanliness that would be necessary through splashing in the water to keep cool. No doubt *pithecanthropus erectus* managed in this way, but we who wear clothes and live in temperate climates have not as much instinct towards cleanliness as health requires, and we therefore have to be taught to wash. The same thing applies to brushing teeth. If we ate our food raw like our remote ancestors, we should not need to brush our teeth, but so long as we retain the unnatural habit of cooking we have to balance it by another unnatural habit, namely the tooth-brush. The "back-to-nature" cult, if it is to be compatible with health, must be thoroughgoing, and must involve the abandonment of clothes and cooking. If we are not prepared to go to these lengths we must teach our children certain habits which they will not acquire for themselves. In the matter of cleanliness and hygiene, therefore, although present conventional education involves much too great a limitation of freedom, yet some limitation is necessary in the interests of health.

35

⅄Another rather humble virtue which is not likely to be produced by a wholly free education is punctuality. Punctuality is a quality the need of which is bound up with social co-operation. It has nothing to do with the relation of the soul to God, or with mystic insight, or with any of the matters with which the more elevated and spiritual moralists are concerned. One would be surprised to find a saint getting drunk, but one would not be surprised to find him late for an engagement. And yet in the ordinary business of life punctuality is absolutely necessary. It would not do for the engine-driver or the postman to wait till the spirit moved him to drive his engine or collect the letters. All economic organizations of any complexity would become unworkable if those concerned were often late. But habits of punctuality are hardly likely to be learned in a free atmosphere. They cannot exist in a man who allows his moods to dominate him. For this reason they are perhaps incompatible with the highest forms of achievement. Newton, as we know, was so unpunctual at his meals that his dog ate them without Newton's ever finding it out. The highest achievement in most directions demands capacity for absorption in a mood, but those whose work is less skilled, from royalty downward, do much harm if they are habitually unpunctual. It seems unavoidable, therefore, that young people should be subjected to the necessity of doing certain things at certain times if they are to be fitted to take any ordinary part in modern life. Those who show extraordinary talent, as poets or composers or pure mathematicians, may be exempted, but 99 per cent. of mankind need a discipline in observing time which is quite impossible if they are allowed to grow freely as their natural impulses dictate. The noble savage, one presumes, went hunting when he was hungry, and not at 8.53 a.m. like his descendant in the suburbs. The education of the noble savage, therefore, does not supply all that the dweller in the suburbs requires.

A rather more serious matter, to which similar considerations apply, is honesty. I do not mean this term in any fancy sense; I mean merely respect for the property of others. This is not a natural characteristic of human beings. The undisciplined human being appropriates the property of others whenever he considers it safe to do so. Perhaps even the disciplined human being does this not infrequently, but discipline has taught him that theft is often not safe when at first sight it seems so. There is, I think, in the minds of some humane moderns a certain confusion of thought on this subject. Having discovered that there is such a thing as kleptomania, they are inclined to regard all thieving as kleptomania. But this is quite a mistake. Kleptomania consists of stealing things, which often the thief does not really want, in circumstances where he is pretty sure to be caught. It has as a rule some psychological source: the kleptomaniac,

37

unconsciously to himself, is stealing love, or objects having some sexual significance. Kleptomania cannot be dealt with by punishment, but only by psychological understanding. Ordinary thieving, however, is by no means irrational, and just because it is rational it can be prevented by being made contrary to self-interest through social penalties. In a community of children whom their elders leave free, the thief, unless he is the biggest of the group, will be severely punished by the others. The elders may wash their hands of the punishment and say that in their system there is no penal code, but in this they are guilty of self-deception. The chances are that the penal code spontaneously created by a group of children will be more severe and more unreliable than one invented by adults. For the sake of the thief himself, therefore, it is on the whole wise that adults should take cognizance of acts of theft, and deal with them in a manner which prevents the other children from wreaking vengeance on their own account. An adequate respect for the property of others is hardly possible except through the creation of a conditioned reflex. Under the influence of temptation the chance of detection always appears less than it is, and the person to whom thieving is an active possibility is hardly likely to go through life without yielding to the temptation sufficiently often to be caught in the end.

Another respect in which, to my mind, many

apostles of freedom go astray, is that they fail to ,
recognize sufficiently the importance of routine in
the life of the young. I do not mean that a routine
should be rigid and absolute : there should be days
when it is varied, such as Christmas Day and
holidays. But even these variations should, on the
whole, be expected by the child. A life of uncer-
tainty is nervously exhausting at all times, but
especially in youth. The child derives a sense of
security from knowing more or less what is going
to happen day by day. He wishes his world to be
safe, and subject to the reign of law. Our belief in
the uniformity of nature is largely the projection
upon the cosmos of the child's desire for routine
in the nursery. Adventurousness and courage are
highly desirable qualities, but they are most easily
developed against a background of fundamental
security.

A further point in favour of a large element of
routine is that children find it both tiring and boring
to have to choose their own occupation at all odd
times. They prefer that at many times the initiative
should not be theirs, and that their own choice
should be confined within a framework imposed
by friendly adults. Children, like grown-ups, enjoy
the sense of achievement derived from mastering
a difficulty, but this requires a consistency of effort
of which few are capable without some outside
encouragement. The capacity for consistent self-
direction is one of the most valuable that a human

39

being can possess. It is practically unknown in young children, and is never developed either by a very rigid discipline or by complete freedom. Very rigid discipline, such as that of soldiers in war-time, makes a man incapable of acting without the goad of external command. On the other hand, complete freedom throughout childhood does not teach him to resist the solicitations of a momentary impulse: he does not acquire the capacity of concentrating upon one matter when he is interested in another, or of resisting pleasures because they will cause fatigue that will interfere with subsequent work. The strengthening of the will demands, therefore, a somewhat subtle mixture of freedom and discipline, and is destroyed by an excess of either.

What is important as imposing limitations upon the desirable amount of discipline is that all training should have the co-operation of the child's will, though not of every passing impulse. Every child who is surrounded by friendly adults is conscious at bottom that he himself is rather foolish, and is grateful for a fair amount of guidance from those whom he can trust to be really concerned with his good, and not only with their own convenience or power. Athletes submit themselves to discipline as a matter of course, and young people whose desire for intellectual achievement is as great as the athlete's desire for success in his field will be equally ready to submit themselves to the necessary discipline.

40

But in an atmosphere where all discipline is thought evil, it will not occur to young people that voluntary submission of this sort is an essential of almost every kind of success. Difficult success as an ideal should be present to the mind of the young if they are not to become wayward and futile. But there are few to whom it will occur in an environment where freedom is absolute.

The use of authority as opposed to persuasion can be reduced almost to nothing where the right sort of adult is in charge of not too large a number of children. Take, for example, such a matter as kindliness. I do not think that precept or punishment can do anything to produce a kindly disposition, though it can restrain overt acts of cruelty. A kindly disposition requires, on the one hand, instinctive happiness, and on the other hand the example of kindly behaviour on the part of adults. The mere teaching of kindliness as a moral principle is, to my mind, almost useless.

It is of the highest importance that whatever discipline may exist should not involve more than a minimum of emotional restraint, for a child who feels himself thwarted in any important way is liable to develop various undesirable characteristics the nature of which will depend upon his strength of character. If he is strong, he will become an angry rebel, while if he is weak he will become a whining hypocrite. Discipline, therefore, while it cannot be entirely absent, should be reduced as

41

much as is compatible with the training of decent
and competent human beings.

The matter of instruction is the crux of the whole
question. Experience has persuaded me, somewhat
to my surprise, that it is possible to give adequate
instruction, and to produce highly educated human
beings, without imposing any obligation to be
present at lessons. To do this requires a combina-
tion of circumstances which is not at present possible on a large scale. It requires among adults a
genuine and spontaneous interest in intellectual
pursuits. It requires small classes. It requires sympathy and tact and skill in the teacher. And it
requires an environment in which it is possible to
turn a child out of a class and tell him to go and
play, if he wishes to be in class solely for the purpose of creating a disturbance. It will be a long
time before these conditions can be realized in
ordinary schools, and therefore, for the present,
compulsory attendance in class is likely to be necessary in the great majority of cases.

There are some who argue that if a child is left
alone he will teach himself to read and write and
so forth from a wish not to be inferior to his neighbours, and that therefore absence of compulsion
causes at most a delay of a year or two in the
acquisition of knowledge. I think that this position
is unconsciously parasitic. In a world where every
other child learns to read and write, it is probable
that any given child will in time wish to escape the

sense of inferiority which would be produced by ignorance. But in a world where all children escaped compulsion, there would soon be no occasion for this sense of inferiority, and each generation would be somewhat more ignorant than its predecessor. Very few children have a spontaneous impulse to learn the multiplication table. While their neighbours are compelled to learn it, they may, for very shame, feel that they ought to learn it too, but in a community where no child was obliged to learn it there would, before long, be only a few erudite pedants who would know what six times nine is.

The acquisition of concrete knowledge is pleasant to most children: if they live on a farm they will watch the farmer's operations and get to know all about them. But abstract knowledge is loved by very few, and yet it is abstract knowledge that makes a civilized community possible. Preservation of a civilized community demands, therefore, some method of causing children to behave in a manner which is not natural to them. It may be possible to substitute coaxing for compulsion, but it is not possible to leave the matter to the unaided operation of nature. The idea of education as merely affording opportunities for natural growth is not, I think, one which can be upheld by a person who realizes the complexity of modern societies. It is, of course, possible to say that this complexity is regrettable, and that it would be better to return

43

to a simpler way of life, but unfortunately the process of so returning would involve the death by starvation of a very large percentage of the population. This alternative is so horrible that we are practically committed to the whole complex apparatus of the modern industrial world, and being so committed, we are also bound to fit our children to take their part in carrying it on. The negative theory of education, therefore, while it has many important elements of truth, and is largely valid so far as the emotions are concerned, cannot be accepted in its entirety as regards intellectual and technical training. Where these are concerned, something more positive is required.

CHAPTER III

EDUCATION AND HEREDITY

THE character of an adult plant or animal results
from the interaction of the environment and the
organism from the moment of fertilization onwards.
I have tried to make this statement as colourless
and uncontroversial as possible, because everything
more definite is matter of controversy. The proportion of heredity and environment in forming
an adult human character is very differently estimated by different authorities. Among men of
science there is a natural tendency for heredity
to be emphasized by geneticists, while environment
is emphasized by psychologists. There is, however,
another line of cleavage on this question, not scientific, but political. Conservatives and imperialists
lay stress on heredity because they belong to the
white race but are rather uneducated. Radicals
lay stress on education because it is potentially
democratic, and because it gives a reason for ignor-
ing difference of colour. This political cleavage on
the whole overrides that of geneticist and psycho-
logist. Hogben, though a geneticist, finds little to
be said in favour of eugenics, while governmental
psychologists, such as Goddard and Terman, tend
to emphasize heredity. Americans of this school
always tacitly assume the superiority of the Nordics,

though even the most conservative among them are constrained to admit that the mountaineers of North Carolina and Kentucky, who are of pure English and Scottish descent, none the less have, on the average, lower intelligence quotients than are found among Jewish immigrants.

Where there is so large a margin of controversy, let us first of all establish some indubitable limiting points. Even the most ardent believers in education do not deny that the children of human beings are human, and are more educable than animals; nor do they question such obvious facts as that the children of white people are white, while the children of black people are black. *Per contra*, the devotees of heredity do not deny that a promising child may be ruined by *encephalitis lethargica*, or that it is bad for a child's intelligence to give it opium from infancy, as many ignorant mothers do. Such points of agreement do not, however, take us very far.

When the question is considered scientifically a difficulty arises through the fact that parents, who transmit the hereditary elements, are usually also a very important part of the environment. Similarities of behaviour between parents and children are as likely to be due to imitation as to heredity. For this reason, children in orphan asylums should afford good material, but unfortunately the information available concerning their parents is apt to be very fragmentary. Studies of identical twins have been made with a view to showing the strength of congenital elements,[1] but unfortunately identical twins usually have a close similarity in their environment. It is to be hoped that some scientific millionaire will found a trust for separating identical twins at birth, and bringing them up in widely differing circumstances. I do not believe that if a Queen gave birth to identical twins, one of whom was brought up in the Palace, and the other in a slum, their mental similarity at the age of twenty would be very close; but in the absence of experiment I must admit that my opinion is scarcely scientific. It was formerly believed that there was a princely mode of behaviour which depended on royal blood. Herodotus relates that Cyrus, after being brought up as a peasant from birth to the age of twelve, was recognized by his grandfather on account of his kingly bearing. I doubt, however, whether even the most extreme believers in Nordic superiority would regard this story as plausible.

The powers of education have been exaggerated just as much as the powers of heredity. Dr. John B. Watson apparently believes that any child, by a suitable education, can be turned into a Mozart or a Newton; unfortunately, however, he has not yet told us what sort of education this should be. In his belief in the omnipotence of education he is by no means an innovator. Take, for example, Godwin, the author of *Political Justice* and the father-

[1] See Lange, *Crime as Destiny*, translated by Mrs. J. B. S. Haldane.

in-law of Shelley. His statements on this subject are unequivocal: "It is not improbable, if it should be found that the capacity of the scull [*sic*] of a wise man is greater than that of a fool, that this enlargement should be produced by the incessantly repeated action of the intellectual faculties, especially if we recollect of how flexible materials the sculls of infants are composed, and at how early an age persons of eminent intellectual merit acquire some portion of their future characteristics." "The essential differences that are to be found between individual and individual, originate in the opinions they form, and the circumstances by which they are controled [*sic*]. It is impossible to believe that the same moral training would not make nearly the same man. Let us suppose a being to have heard all the arguments and been subject to all the excitements that were ever addressed to any celebrated character. The same arguments, with all their strength and all their weakness, unaccompanied with the smallest addition or variation, and retailed in exactly the same proportions from month to month and year to year, must surely have produced the same opinions. The same excitements, without reservation, whether direct or accidental, must have fixed the same propensities. Whatever science or pursuit was selected by this celebrated character, must be loved by the person respecting whom we are supposing this identity of impressions. In fine, it is impression that makes the man, and,

48

compared with the empire of impression, the mere differences of animal structure are inexpressibly un-important and powerless." Substitute "conditioned reflexes" for "opinions," and "stimuli" for "argu-ments," and you have a passage that (except as regards style) might have been written by Dr. Watson.

Against this view of the omnipotence of education there are many arguments. Godwin's view that the habit of thinking enlarges the skull is not one which any modern would advocate; this, however, is not conclusive, since no clear correlation has been established between intelligence and size of brain, except in extreme cases. Idiocy is often connected with a congenital malformation of the skull, and I imagine that even Dr. Watson would not regard idiocy as due to bad education. The case of low-grade mentally deficients is only one degree less evident. At the other extreme, take the example of calculating boys:[1] it is impossible to imagine anything in the environment which could cause one of a set of brothers to be able to take cube roots of large numbers in his head with no more ostensible training in arithmetic than falls to the lot of the average boy. If it be granted that the idiot and the calculating boy are congenitally different from the average, it seems highly improbable that there are not other less extreme congenital variations.

[1] For a brief account of them, see Hollingworth, *Gifted Children*, pp. 210–216.

While it is dangerous to trust to unscientific impressions, (I think some weight must be allowed to the experience of practical educators, none of whom, so far as I have been able to discover, have any doubt that there are differences of native ability among their pupils. It is admittedly difficult, if not impossible, to determine what is due to heredity and what to environment; but that some part of the difference of intelligence between one adult and another is congenital is, in my opinion, nearly certain.)

There is, however, both in Godwin and in Dr. John B. Watson, an argument by which they profess to prove their thesis. The argument is that human beings do not have instincts, and that therefore the mind of a child has no character independent of experience. One might retort to Dr. Watson by an argument from authority: Pavlov asserts that his dogs exhibit the four kinds of temperament enumerated by Hippocrates, and suffer from different types of nervous disorder according to the kind to which they belong. Dr. Watson might, however, reply that these differences of temperament may have been caused by circumstances of which Pavlov was not aware, and that all dogs are born equal. We must, therefore, meet his theoretical argument.

Let it be granted, for the sake of argument, that unconditioned reflexes (which have replaced instincts) are the same in all new-born infants. Does it follow that there can be no congenital mental differences? Surely not. Take the learning of conditioned reflexes : some will learn more quickly than others, some will learn more effectively to discriminate between stimuli that only differ slightly. Even if we grant that all education consists in the formation of conditioned reflexes, which is a disputable proposition, it still does not follow that all children are equally educable. The position of the extreme advocates of education as against heredity has, therefore, no better foundation in theory than in practical observation.

But although the importance of congenital differences among human beings cannot be denied, the practical inferences drawn by eugenists are for the most part quite unscientific. No one knows what factors making for socially desirable qualities are hereditary, nor which of such factors are respectively dominant and recessive. There is not even any agreement as to what is socially desirable. From a very limited observation I am inclined to think that there is some correlation between excellence in pictorial art and incompetence in arithmetic. Assuming this to be the case, what should the eugenist do about it? Should he produce a race of painters who cannot do accounts, or a race of accountants who are indifferent to art? The recognized intelligence tests are not without value in their own province, but they do nothing to test either moral or artistic qualities. Neither the

51

ethical nor the scientific foundations are sufficiently secure for any practical eugenic measures, except, possibly, the sterilization of the feeble-minded. The following assumptions are unwarranted:

That negroes are congenitally inferior to white men;

That persons born in Asia are inferior to those born in Europe or America;

That Europeans born north of latitude 45° are congenitally superior to those born south of that latitude;

That persons whose fathers have above £1,000 a year are a better stock than those whose fathers have less.

All these propositions are believed by most eugenists, and the first three have influenced the immigration laws of the United States.

If the subject of the inheritance of ability is to be treated scientifically, there will be need of a great deal of preliminary work. There will be, first of all, the need of discovering measurable mental qualities which do not depend upon education. The intelligence tests are intended to do this, but they only do it, at best, within a homogeneous social milieu. There are questions about money, for example, which will be answered more readily by urban than by rural children. There are questions demanding rhymes to certain words, which will be easier for children educated in poetry than for others. As soon as the intelligence tests are applied to the comparison of children with widely differing backgrounds, they become quite misleading; yet it is by just such applications that many believers in heredity as against environment obtain their results.

So long as children live with their parents, it is impossible to separate hereditary and educational factors in any mental similarity which may exist. If the whole population were subjected to intelligence tests, valuable material would, in time, be obtainable from orphan asylums. If it were found that, in a given asylum, there was a correlation between the intelligence of children and that of their parents, that would be good evidence of heredity. But at present such evidence is still to be sought.

In seeking laws of mental heredity, the quality selected should be simple, definite, and measurable. One might, for example, utter a sentence, preferably nonsensical, and demand that the child should repeat it. The number of words in the longest sentence that a child could repeat correctly would measure a mental quality, though not necessarily a very desirable one. Macaulay, as every one knows, possessed this quality to an almost incredible degree; but unfortunately there is no evidence as to whether his father or mother possessed it. If all school children were tested in this respect on each birthday throughout their school years, we might, within forty years, acquire material of considerable value as regards mental heredity.

53

Such statistical methods, however, will never satisfy the Mendelian, who wishes to isolate the particular gene or group of genes concerned in any instance of heredity. Mental qualities are so complex that this seems, for a long time to come, a hopeless task. It is possible, however, that some mental qualities may be more capable of isolation than are most of the others. Mathematical and musical ability both suggest themselves as suitable in this respect. Both are statistically rare, but, where they exist, are liable to be enormously in excess of the average. Both tend to run in families, but it is impossible to know how far this is due to education. Mozart, for example, had a musical father, but his father transmitted musical instruction as well as musical ability. So far as I know, no great musical or mathematical genius has ever come out of an orphan asylum, so that this method of testing heredity fails us.

The work of Galton and his followers, designed to prove that ability is inherited, is far from scientifically convincing, although it is probable that there is some truth in their thesis. But until ways have been devised for eliminating the effect of the parental environment, the whole subject must remain open to doubt.

The outcome of the matter, from the standpoint of the practical educator, is simple. It is to be expected that there will be differences of ability among pupils, which are not traceable to the influence of environment; whatever native talent is discovered should be cultivated, and, if really remarkable, should be allowed, from an early age, to take up time which would otherwise be given to general education. But nothing whatever should be presumed either for or against the intelligence of a pupil or group of pupils on account of the race or social status or personal achievements of their parents. There is room for investigation as to the inheritance of ability, and it is easy to devise methods by which the matter could be studied scientifically; but if such methods were adopted it would necessarily be at least a generation before they could bear fruit, and in the meantime the only scientifically sound position is to confess our ignorance as to the distribution of native ability and the laws of its inheritance.

CHAPTER IV

EMOTION AND DISCIPLINE

EDUCATION has at all times had a twofold aim, namely instruction and training in good conduct. The conception of good conduct varies with the political institutions and social traditions of the community. In the middle ages, when there was a hierarchical organization proceeding from the serf by gradual stages up to God, the chief virtue was obedience. Children were taught to obey their parents and to reverence their social superiors, to feel awe in the presence of the priest and submission in the presence of the Lord of the Manor. Only the Emperor and the Pope were free, and, since the morality of the time afforded no guidance to free men, they spent their time in fighting each other. The moderns differ from the men of the thirteenth century both in aim and in method. (Democracy has substituted co-operation for submission and herd-instinct for reverence; the group in regard to which herd-instinct is to be most operative has become the nation, which was formerly rendered unimportant by the universality of the Church. Meanwhile propaganda has become persuasive rather than forceful, and has learnt to proceed by the instilling of suitable sentiments in early youth. Church music, school songs, and the flag determine, by their influence on

56

the boy, the subsequent actions of the man in moments of strong emotion. Against these influences the assaults of reason have but little power.

The influence of political conceptions on early education is not always obvious, and is often unconscious on the part of the educator. For the present, therefore, I wish to consider education in behaviour with as little regard as possible to the social order, to which I shall return at a later stage.

When it is sought to produce a certain kind of behaviour in a child or animal, there are two different techniques which may be followed. We may, on the one hand, by means of rewards and punishments cause the child or animal to perform or abstain from certain precise acts; or we may, on the other hand, seek to produce in the child or animal such emotions as will lead, on the whole, to acts of the kind desired.

By a suitable distribution of rewards and punishments, it is possible to control a very large part of overt behaviour.

Usually the only form of reward or punishment required will be praise or blame. By this method boys who are naturally timid can acquire physical courage, and children who are sensitive to pain can be taught a stoical endurance. Good manners, if not imposed earlier, can be learnt in adolescence by means of no worse punishment than the contemptuous lifting of an eyebrow. What is called "good form" is acquired by almost all who are exposed to it, merely

57

from fear of the bad opinion incurred by infringing it. Those who have been taught from an early age to fear the displeasure of their group as the worst of misfortunes will die on the battlefield, in a war of which they understand nothing, rather than suffer the contempt of fools. The English public schools have carried this system to perfection, and have largely sterilized intelligence by making it cringe before the herd. This is what is called making a boy manly.

(As a social force, the behaviourist method of "conditioning" is therefore very powerful and very successful. It can and does cause men to act in ways quite different from those in which they would otherwise have acted, and it is capable of producing an impressive uniformity of overt behaviour. Nevertheless, it has its limitations.

It was through Freud that these limitations first became known in a scientific manner, though men of psychological insight had long ago perceived them in an intuitive way. For our purposes, the essential discovery of psycho-analysis is this ⟨that an impulse which is prevented, by behaviourist methods, from finding overt expression in action, does not necessarily die, but is driven underground, and finds some new outlet which has not been inhibited by training. Often the new outlet will be more harmful than the one that has been prevented, and in any case the deflection involves emotional disturbance and unprofitable expenditure of energy. It is therefore necessary to pay more attention to emotion, as opposed to overt behaviour, than is done by those who advocate conditioning as alone sufficient in the training of character.

There are, moreover, some undesirable habits in regard to which the method of rewards and punishments fails completely, even from its own point of view. One of these is bed-wetting. When this persists beyond the age at which it usually stops, punishment only makes it more obstinate. Although this fact has long been known to psychologists, it is still unknown to most schoolmasters, who for years on end punish boys having this habit, without ever noticing that the punishment does not produce reform. The cause of the habit, in older boys, is usually some deep-seated unconscious psychological disturbance, which must be brought to the surface before a cure can be effected.

The same kind of psychological mechanism applies in many less obvious instances. In the case of definite nervous disorders this is now widely recognized. Kleptomania, for example, is not uncommon in children, and, unlike ordinary thieving, it cannot be cured by punishment, but only by ascertaining and removing its psychological cause. What is less recognized is that we all suffer, to a greater or less degree, from nervous disorders having an emotional origin. A man is called sane when he is as sane as the average of his contemporaries; but in the average man many of the mechanisms which determine his opinions and actions are quite fantastic, so much so that in a world of real sanity they would be called insane. It is dangerous to produce good social behaviour by means which leave the anti-social emotions untouched. So long as these emotions, while persisting, are denied all outlet, they will grow stronger and stronger, leading to impulses of cruelty which will at last become irresistible. In the man of weak will, these impulses may break out in crime, or in some form of behaviour to which social penalties are attached. In the man of strong will, they take even more undesirable forms. He may be a tyrant in the home, ruthless in business, bellicose in politics, persecuting in his social morality; for all these qualities other men with similar defects of character will admire him; he will die universally respected, after having spread hatred and misery over a city, a nation, or an epoch according to his ability and his opportunities. (Correct behaviour combined with bad emotions is not enough, therefore, to make a man a contributor to the happiness of mankind. If this is our criterion of desirable conduct, something more must be sought in the education of character.)

Such considerations, as well as the sympathetic observation of children, suggest that the (behaviourist method of training character is inadequate, and needs to be supplemented by a quite different method.)

Experience of children shows that it is possible to operate upon feeling, and not only upon outward
60

behaviour, by giving children an environment in which desirable emotions shall become common and undesirable emotions rare. Some children (and some adults) are of a cheerful disposition, others are morose; some are easily contented with any pleasure that offers, while others are inconsolable unless they can have the particular pleasure on which their hearts are set; some, in the absence of evidence, regard the bulk of human beings with friendly confidence, while others regard most people with terrified suspicion. The prevalent emotional attitude of the child generally remains that of the adult, though in later life men learn to conceal their timidities and grudges by disguises of greater or lesser effectiveness. It is therefore very important that children should have predominantly those emotional attitudes which, both in childhood and subsequently, will make them happy, successful, and useful, rather than those that lead to unhappiness, failure, and malevolence. There is no doubt that it is within the power of psychology to determine the kind of environment that promotes desirable emotions, and that often intelligent affection without science can arrive at the right result. When this method is rightly used, its effect on character is more radical and far more satisfactory than the effect to be obtained by rewards and punishments.

The right emotional environment for a child is a delicate matter, and of course varies with the child's age. Throughout childhood, though to a continually

61

diminishing extent, there is need of the feeling of
safety. For this purpose, kindness and a pleasant
routine are the essentials. The relation with adults
should be one of play and physical ease, but not of
emotional caresses. There should be close intimacy
with other children. Above all, there should be
opportunity for initiative in construction, in exploration, and in intellectual and artistic directions.
The child has two opposite needs, safety and freedom, of which the latter gradually grows at the
expense of the former. The affection given by adults
should be such as to cause a feeling of safety, but
not such as to limit freedom or to arouse a deep
emotional response in the child. Play, which is a
vital need of childhood, should be contributed not
only by other children, but also by parents, and is
essential to the best relation between parents and
children.

Freedom is the most difficult element to secure
under existing conditions. I am not an advocate of
absolute freedom, for reasons which we considered
in an earlier chapter; but (I am an advocate of
certain forms of freedom which most adults find
unendurable. There should be no enforced respect
for grown-ups, who should allow themselves to be
called fools whenever children wish to call them so.
We cannot prevent our children from thinking us
fools by merely forbidding them to utter their
thoughts; in fact, they are more likely to think ill
of us if they dare not say so. Children should not be

forbidden to swear—not because it is desirable that they should swear, but because it is desirable that they should think that it does not matter whether they do or not, since this is a true proposition. They should be free entirely from the sex taboo, and not checked when their conversation seems to inhibited adults to be indecent. If they express opinions on religion or politics or morals, they may be met with argument, provided it is genuine argument, but not if it is really dogma: the adult may, and should, suggest considerations to them, but should not impose conclusions.

Given such conditions, children may grow up fearless and fundamentally happy, without the resentment that comes of thwarting or the excessive demands that are produced by an atmosphere of hothouse affection. Their intelligence will be untrammelled, and their views on human affairs will have the kindliness that comes of contentment. A world of human beings with this emotional equipment would make short work of our social system, with its wars, its oppressions, its economic injustice, its horror of free speech and free inquiry, and its superstitious moral code. The toleration of these evils depends upon timidity in thought and malevolent feeling due to lack of freedom. Dr. Watson, who minimizes the congenital aspects of character, nevertheless allows, as one of the unlearnt reactions of infants, rage at any constriction of the limbs. This instinctive emotion is the basis of the love of freedom.

The man whose tongue is constricted by laws or taboos against free speech, whose pen is constricted by the censorship, whose loves are constricted by an ethic which considers jealousy a better thing than affection, whose childhood has been imprisoned in a code of manners, and whose youth has been drilled in a cruel orthodoxy, will feel against the world that hampers him the same rage that is felt by the infant whose arms and legs are held motionless. In his rage he will turn to destruction, becoming a revolutionary, a militarist, or a persecuting moralist according to temperament and opportunity. To make human beings who will create a better world is a problem in emotional psychology: it is the problem of making human beings who have a free intelligence combined with a happy disposition. This problem is not beyond the powers of science; it is the will, not the power, that is lacking.

CHAPTER V

HOME VERSUS SCHOOL

THAT children should be educated entirely at home is an opinion which is now obsolete, although it is implied in the works of Locke and Rousseau, and was followed in bringing up Alexander, Hannibal, and John Stuart Mill. It is, in fact, only possible as regards the rich, and on this ground alone no longer needs discussion. But the proportions which should exist between home and school, and the age at which children should begin going to school, are legitimate matters of debate.

The view adopted by most European States as regards most of the children of wage-earners is that they should go to day school from the age of six to the age of thirteen or fourteen. A certain percentage of the abler working-class boys and girls are encouraged by scholarships to continue their education beyond that age, while the sons and daughters of the well-to-do do so as a matter of course. There is no agreement as to the age up to which it would be desirable, apart from difficulties due to public expense, to carry universal education; nor is there any agreement as to whether day schools or boarding schools are preferable in themselves. It seems to be the general opinion that there is something called the "good home" which is better than any boarding school, but that some undefined percentage of homes are not "good" in the sense intended. For my part, I think the question difficult, as there are strong arguments on different sides. The question is really twofold: ((1) At what age should school begin? (2) Should it be day school or boarding school? Let us take these questions in order.)

At what age should school begin? The answer must depend upon the home, but rather upon its topography than upon its moral or psychological character. A child who lives on a farm in the country can happily and profitably spend his time wandering about, watching animals, observing haymaking, reaping, threshing, and ploughing, until the time comes when it is necessary to begin formal instruction. But for the urban child whose parents live in a cramped apartment the matter is quite otherwise. For him, school is desirable as an escape into freedom—freedom of movement, freedom of noise, and freedom of companionship. I have frequently met medical men who opposed nursery schools because they supposed that every school must be a place of instruction with fixed lessons. The right sort of nursery school will have only so much instruction as is necessary in order to keep the children amused. So far from straining children, it should afford them relief from the supervision and interference which are almost unavoidable in small homes.

Urban children whose parents are not rich have

{certain needs, physical and psychological, which cannot be satisfied at home.\The first of these is light and air. Margaret McMillan found that a very large percentage of the children at her nursery school had rickets when they first came, and that almost all recovered by being in the open air. The second need is proper diet. This is not expensive, and could in theory be supplied at home, but in practice this is impossible owing to lack of knowledge and culinary conservatism. The third need is space in which to romp and play. The children of the very poor find this in the street, but others are forbidden to do so. And in any case the street is not the best place for play. The fourth need is noise. It is cruel to a child to forbid him to make a noise, but in most homes several noisy children at once can make life intolerable for the grown-ups. The fifth need is the companionship of other children of about the same age, a need which begins towards the end of the second year, and rapidly increases. The sixth need is escape from parental interest; this is a more important factor where the well-to-do are concerned than it is with the poorer classes, in which mothers are usually too busy to do as much harm to their children as middle-class mothers do by constant observation, however intelligent and benevolent. The seventh need is an environment containing appropriate amusements, but artificially safe, i.e. without such things as stone steps or sharp corners or valuable fragile objects. Children deprived of all

67

these needs until the age of six are likely to be sickly, unenterprising, and nervous.

The problem of the care of young children in large towns is one to which the modern State, with the exception of the municipality of Vienna, is not yet alive. It is largely an architectural question. In the poorer quarters of cities, apartments should be built round three sides of a courtyard, leaving the south open to the sun. The centre space should be devoted to the children, who should play and eat there under supervision, returning to their parents for sleep. This would at once relieve the mothers and immensely benefit the children. But at present the individualism of the separate home stands in the way, especially in England, where it dominates architecture more than in any other country.

It must, I suppose, be assumed that the rich would not allow their children to share the joys of such communal playgrounds. But it is as important for the children of the rich as for those of the poor to escape into freedom for a great part of the day. No urban home, however excellent, can supply what is necessary for the healthy mental and physical growth of a child. Social selectness can be secured by high fees, but some form of nursery school is essential in any class.

So far, we have been considering what are called the pre-school years. As children grow older, the arguments in favour of boarding schools grow stronger. Much the weightiest of these arguments is that boarding schools can be in the country in the best surroundings, whereas day schools, for most children, must be in the town. Another argument, which applies in many cases though not in all, is that home is apt to be a place where a child is subjected to nervous strain. It may be that the parents quarrel, that the mother is over-anxious, that the father is unkind; there may be a favoured brother or sister, who causes the others to suffer from jealousy; either parent may be injudiciously affectionate. In one way or another, home is often too emotional. Children need a quiet life, containing enjoyments and activities, but few intense emotions. As against all this, it must, I think, be conceded that a due amount of wise parental affection is good for a child, giving him a sense of security and of his worth as a human being. Between these opposing considerations it is not easy to strike a balance.

The question of home versus school is difficult to argue in the abstract. If ideal homes are contrasted with actual schools, the balance tips one way; if ideal schools are contrasted with actual homes, the balance tips the other way. I have no doubt in my own mind that the ideal school is better than the ideal home, at any rate the ideal urban home, because it allows more light and air, more freedom of·movement, and more companionship of contemporaries. But it by no means follows that the actual school will be better than the actual home. The majority of parents feel affection for their

69

children, and this sets limits to the harm they do them. But education authorities have no affection for the children concerned; at best, they are actuated by public spirit, which is directed towards the community as a whole, and not merely towards the children; at worst, they are politicians engaged in squabbles for plums. At present, the home plays an important part in forming the mentality of the young, a part by no means wholly good, but perhaps better than that which would be played by the State if it were in sole control of children. Home gives the child experience of affection, and of a small community in which he is important; also of relations with people of both sexes and different ages, and of the multifarious business of adult life. In this way it is useful as a corrective of the artificial simplification of school.

Another merit of home is that it preserves the diversity between individuals. If we were all alike, it might be convenient for the bureaucrat and the statistician, but it would be very dull, and would lead to a very unprogressive society. At present, the differences between individuals are greatly accentuated by the differences between their homes. Too much difference is a barrier to social solidarity, but some difference is essential to the best form of cooperation. An orchestra requires men with different talents and, within certain limits, different tastes; if all men insisted upon playing the trombone, orchestral music would be impossible. Social co-

70

operation, in like manner, requires differences of taste and aptitude, which are less likely to exist if all children are exposed to exactly the same influences than if parental differences are allowed to affect them. This is to my mind an important argument against the Platonic doctrine that children should be wholly reared by the State.

In the world as it is at present there are two agencies, outside the family, which are concerned with young people: the State is only one of them, the other being the Churches. In England, among the children of wage-earners, about two-thirds are educated by the State, but the remainder are divided between different religious bodies, chiefly Anglicans and Roman Catholics. The children of the well-to-do are mainly educated in an Anglican atmosphere. Most of the "best" girls' schools are Anglo-Catholic, and the hold of religion on upper- and middle-class education is increasing.

Both Church and State, as at present constituted, have certain defects as influences in education. I shall be considering these defects at length in later chapters, and will only say, by way of anticipation, that both Church and State demand assent to propositions which no unbiassed person can believe, and to a morality which is so cruel that it can only be accepted by those whose kindliness has been inhibited by dogma. Of incredible propositions, the following may serve as examples. The Roman Catholic Church holds that a priest can turn a

71

piece of bread into the Body and Blood of Christ by talking Latin to it; the British State holds that the Empire is a boon to subject nations. In order to cause young people to believe such propositions, it is necessary to keep them stupid, and to teach them not to use their powers of reasoning in certain directions. Of a cruel morality, the following are instances. The Roman Catholic Church demands legislation such that, if a woman becomes pregnant by a syphilitic man, she must not artificially interrupt her pregnancy, but must allow a probably syphilitic child to be born, in order that, after a few years of misery on earth, it may spend eternity in limbo (assuming its parents to be not Catholics). The British State considers it the duty of an Englishman to kill people who are not English whenever a collection of elderly gentlemen in Westminster tells him to do so. Such instances suffice to illustrate the fact that Church and State are implacable enemies of both intelligence and virtue.

It is therefore dangerous to diminish the influence of home in education until we know what is going to take its place. Given a world State emancipated from theology, it is probable that the home would be of much less value to young people, and that they would, on the average, become both happier and more intelligent through the removal of parental influences. But at present, except in Russia, all progress has to be won in opposition to Church and State, and anything that increases their hold over men's minds is to be viewed with alarm.

The question whether children should be removed from parents and brought up by the State must be considered, not only in relation to children, but also in relation to parents. The parental sentiment has a powerful influence upon behaviour, not only in women, but also in men. We have not the data to enable us to judge what men and women would be like if this sentiment were removed, but we may safely conjecture that they would be greatly changed. It is probable that most women would feel little desire for children in such circumstances, and that child-bearing would have to become a paid profession, adopted as a branch of the civil service. It is probable that the relations of men and women would grow trivial, and that serious conjugal affection would become rare. It is probable that men would become less inclined to work hard, since at present, in middle life, the chief incentive of many men is desire to provide for their families. This is proved by the heavy payments men make for life insurance, which show that they care what happens to their families after they are dead. It may be doubted whether, in a world where the family did not exist, ordinary men would concern themselves with events occurring after their death. It is possible that a kind of paralysis would descend upon the community, such as descends upon a hive of bees when the queen is removed. As to this, only

73

experience can decide, and as yet experience is lacking.

There is, however, a great deal to be said on the other side. All possessive emotions are dangerous, and not least those of parents for their children. The feelings of parents for their children are intensely individualistic and competitive; many men who, while they are childless, are full of public spirit become absorbed in the welfare of their own family as soon as they become fathers. The passion for private property is largely bound up with the family, and communists, from Plato downwards, are right in thinking that their economic system demands the cessation of private property in children. It is possible that whatever is admirable and useful in the parental sentiment could be transferred to the children in a given school, or, in exceptional individuals, to children in general. This, if it could be done, would be a definite moral advance. The parental sentiment is, I believe, the chief source of altruism, and many childless women have shown how valuable it can become when it is universalized. Perhaps, if it could be freed from the possessive taint which it must have while it is associated with actual physical parenthood, the world might lose some of its fierceness, and men might come to wish well to the generality of mankind. All this is conjectural, but it is a hypothesis which should be borne in mind.

The question of home versus school is one which,

up to a certain point, can be decided on a basis of common sense without raising fundamental issues. But when we try to pass beyond that point we are met by our ignorance of human psychology: we do not know how much in our sentiments is instinctive, or how vigorous our sentiments could be if they were trained to be quite other than they are at present. It is to be hoped that Russia will in time supply data which will enable us to know more on these questions; in the meantime, the only scientific attitude is one of suspense of judgement.

CHAPTER VI

ARISTOCRATS, DEMOCRATS, AND BUREAUCRATS

THE family and the State have been opposing forces ever since the State first existed: only in the Royal Family could the two harmonize emotionally. Consequently a pretence arose that the nation was a large family, of which the sovereign was the head. This view prevailed in China and Japan, in Mexico and Peru, and to some extent wherever the conception of divine kingship was strong. By such means a strong State could be created: the sentiment which made men loyal was partly religious veneration and partly respect for the head of the family. The impersonal State was a creation of the Greeks and Romans, especially the latter: the elder Brutus sacrificing his sons for the public good is a story embodying what may be called the religion of public spirit. In the East, this religion is quite recent, and a product of European influences. Confucius deliberately put filial piety above the law, and blamed a son who surrendered a criminal father to justice. In Japan, patriotism still has a great deal of the ancient character of devotion to the divine Head of the Family; when, as must happen, this sentiment decays under the influence of rationalism, it is doubtful whether the Japanese

76

polity will survive, and it is not improbable that it may give place to a government more on the Russian model. In China there has been a persistent attempt to create a modern patriotism in place of the old family feeling; this attempt has centred round the Kuo Min Tang party and the almost religious veneration for Sun Yat-sen. In India a modern patriotism is arising through hatred of the English. But in all these countries, since they lack the Roman tradition, patriotism as we understand it is still somewhat exotic.

In modern times the closest approach to the Roman sentiment has existed in the British upper class. Elsewhere, until the French Revolution, the State was personified in the monarch; in England, after the execution of Charles I, the State and the monarch were sharply separated in men's minds. Throughout the period from 1688 to 1832, England was, in effect, a patrician republic, in which the ruling families had that almost instinctive understanding of public affairs that had characterized the Romans in their great days. I do not mean that either in England or in Rome the aristocracy showed any indifference to their private interests. The younger Brutus, that model of stern republican virtue, lent money to a municipality at 60 per cent., and when they failed to pay the interest he hired a private army to besiege them. The English aristocracy of the eighteenth century used their control over both Houses of Parliament to rob

77

common people of their rights by means of the Enclosure Acts. Nevertheless, in both cases, the governing classes felt the State to be their personal concern, in a way which is scarcely possible for any individual in the vast democracies of the present day.

Every social system has its appropriate educational instrument, which in the case of the British oligarchy was the public school—Eton first and foremost, but also, though in a lesser degree, such schools as Harrow, Winchester, and Rugby. Through the operation of these schools the mentality of the eighteenth-century aristocrat remained that of the holders of political power throughout the nineteenth century, in spite of profound changes in the nominal constitution. The public schools still exist and are still regarded by most well-to-do Englishmen as embodying all that is best in our tradition. It is therefore still necessary to discuss their contribution to our national life.

Psychologically, the most important aspect of the preparatory and public school system is that, at an early age, it removes a boy from home and from all feminine influence, leaving him exposed defenceless to the ill-treatment of older boys and the possible hostility of his contemporaries, compelled to keep to himself all the desire for kindness and mothering which he retains from childhood, and obliged to centre such sentiment as he cannot repress exclusively upon other boys. At first he is likely to be very

78

unhappy, but gradually, if he is not above the average in either sensitiveness or intelligence, he learns to wear an armour and to seem callous; in his school life he aims at power and glory to the exclusion of all other objects; if he is good at athletics he may enjoy a prestige which he will not experience in later life until he has achieved some position of considerable public eminence. In his later years at school the respect of his juniors and his authority over them cause him to forget his initial unhappiness, and by the time he is forty he thinks that his school years were the happiest time of his life. But his happiness, such as it was, came from the exercise of trivial authority and the admiration which he received for unimportant merits. Instinctively he looks about for opportunities of similar enjoyments in later life: he desires people to govern, people to whom he will seem a god-like being. So he goes to live among uncivilized people, or at least people whom he believes to be uncivilized: he becomes an empire-builder, an outpost of culture, a man whose mission it is to bring Western enlightenment into dark places. If the "natives" regard him as the small boys did during his last days at school, all goes well: he is kind and gracious, upright and hard-working, stoical about the loneliness and discomfort, which are no worse than what he endured in his first years at school.

But if the "natives" fail to admire him he begins to present a less pleasant picture. In contact with

79

savages, where his superiority is unquestioned, he
often does well because of his courage and endurance; but in contact with an alien civilization,
such as those of the East, he becomes pitiful. I have
seen in the East men who considered themselves the
fine flower of a public-school education confronted
with learned Orientals, and it made me blush to
be an Englishman. My compatriots might be red-
faced, hard-drinking, spending their working hours
in exploitation and their leisure in sport and bridge,
wholly ignorant of Occidental culture, and not even
aware that any Oriental culture exists. Yet, in
contact with men who knew not only what was
worth knowing in their own civilization, but far
more than most public-school men of the civilization of the West, these ignorant boors would preserve the insolence of military conquerors, content
to let their superiority be proved by the guns of
their warships. To this contemptuous brutality the
Japanese have replied by adopting our standards,
and the rest of the East is following their example.
As an engine of imperialism, the public schools have
failed.

The causes of this failure are partly intellectual,
partly psychological. To begin with the intellectual
causes, which lie nearer the surface: the spirit of
the public schools is one of contempt for intelligence,
and more particularly for scientific intelligence.
Masters are selected largely for their athletic quali-
fications; they must conform, at least outwardly, to

a whole code of behaviour, religious, political, social, and moral, which is intolerable to most intelligent people; they must encourage the boys to be so constantly occupied that they will have no time for sexual sin, and incidentally no time to think; they must discourage whatever traces of mental independence may survive here and there among the cleverer boys; and in the end they must turn out a finished product so imbued with the worship of good form as to be incapable of learning anything important throughout the rest of life. These are a few of the intellectual defects of our public schools—defects inseparable from the fact that the public schools are designed to bolster up a system which is intellectually indefensible.

The psychological defects of the preparatory and public schools are due in the main to two causes, the isolation of the boys from female companionship, and the conventional code of morals. The younger boys at first inevitably miss the affection of mothers and older sisters and even nurses; in these circumstances their mothers often become objects of secret longing and worship, all the more intense because it is *de rigueur* to profess contempt for all women. After puberty they tend to practise masturbation or homosexuality or both, and many of them believe that in so doing they are being sinful. At best they are compelled to be furtive, since all the authorities regard sexual aberrations with horror. This state of affairs tends, in not a few of them, to enhance the mother-image as that of a woman who inspires an affection without carnal taint. This kind of sentiment not infrequently makes happy marriage impossible, and sometimes causes contempt for any woman with whom sexual intercourse is regarded as possible. The unhappiness resulting from this psychological tangle tends to cause cruelty, and to make power the only available source of happiness. The mentality of the imperialist is thus reinforced by the complexes of the sexually starved.

The evils which exist in English public schools are perhaps not all inseparable from aristocratic education, but in the main they are likely to exist wherever there is a class which has hereditary social prominence. Such a class will aim mainly at the power of command; it will therefore cultivate the will rather than intelligence or sensibility, and will include in its training such elements of asceticism as are useful in giving will-power. Under the influence of wealth, aristocracies in the past have frequently become soft from luxury, or yielding from the growth of liberal opinion. Unless these dangers are guarded against, no aristocracy can long maintain itself. Thus both the good and the bad features of the English public schools are necessary in the education of a self-perpetuating aristocratic class. Aristocracy is now out of date, and England, by maintaining it, is coming to be viewed as a curious survival, like the marsupials. For this reason, rather than from any error of detail, Eton no longer has the importance that it had a hundred years ago. Whatever system of education is to fit men to take their place in the modern world, it must not be an aristocratic system.

Democratic education unadulterated has evils which are as great as those of aristocracy, if not greater. (Democracy as a sentiment has two sides. When it says "I am as good as you," it is wholesome; but when it says "you are no better than I am," it becomes oppressive and an obstacle to the development of exceptional merit. To put the matter more accurately: democracy is good when it inspires self-respect, and bad when it inspires persecution of exceptional individuals by the herd. This sort of persecution, of course, exists in aristocratic schools, where exceptional boys are often subjected to grave ill-treatment. It is only under democracy, however, that this sort of thing becomes a theory as well as a practice, and extends beyond the school to the world at large. The toleration of eccentrics, which is one of the best features of English life, is connected with aristocracy. Byron and Shelley suffered social persecution, but less than they would have suffered in a democracy; moreover, they were better able to withstand it than they would have been without aristocratic self-respect.

This, however, is not the chief educational evil of democracy. In America, where democratic sentiment is strong, it is difficult to devise educational

83

systems which give the necessary advantages to clever children. Something has been done in recent times in this direction, but it has been done, in the main, by those who are opposed to democracy. It is clear that some children are more talented than others, and that the more talented, if they are to be as happy and as useful to the community as possible, need different treatment from that which is best for average children. The error of aristocracy lay, not in thinking that some men are superior to others, but in supposing superiority to be hereditary. The error of democracy lies in regarding all claims to superiority as just grounds for the resentment of the herd. In the modern world, much work which is necessary to the community requires more ability than most men possess, and there must be ways of selecting exceptional men to do this work. In general, if they are to be as well qualified as possible, it is desirable to select them while they are still quite young—say twelve years old—and to allow them to make much more rapid progress than is possible to a class of average boys or girls. The feeling that it is undemocratic to single out the best pupils is one which leads to a great waste of good material. We shall deal with this question again in Chapter XII, and I shall therefore say no more about it, except that it is democratic sentiment run wild, not democratic forms of government, that is the cause of the trouble. France is as democratic, politically, as America, but there is no difficulty in securing special treatment for the able, because intellectual and artistic merit is respected, not only when it has achieved a great reputation, but while it is still in process of development.

(Democracy, as a theory, has not the hold on men's minds that it had before the war. It has become evident that, in an industrial society, there are key positions of power, which, if not in the hands of private plutocrats, will be held by officials, who may, remotely, be subject to popular control, but will, in many respects, be able to take important decisions on their own initiative. We thus arrive at bureaucracy as the practical alternative to aristocracy and plutocracy. If everything possible is done to eliminate unjust privilege, power will still be unevenly distributed, because this is unavoidable; but it will be given to those most fitted to exercise it. It will not, however, be irresponsible power, such as belongs to plutocrats and absolute monarchs; it will be power subject to ultimate control by the democracy. Men who are to exercise this sort of power wisely require qualities somewhat different from those produced by either democratic or aristocratic education. The undemocratic element consists in their being avowedly above the average in capacity and knowledge. The unaristocratic element consists in the fact that their position depends, not upon the social status of their fathers, but upon their personal abilities. And since they do not have ultimate and absolute power, they do not need

85

exceptional aptitude for command, but only unusual powers of arriving at sound conclusions, and giving reasons for their conclusions to persons somewhat inferior to themselves in brains.

It is clear that as society grows more organic—which is an effect of modern inventions and technique—the importance of the bureaucrat continually increases. To educate rightly those who are going to be officials is therefore very important in a scientific State. This requires, on the part of educators and educational officials, respect for native intelligence in children and means of detecting it; it requires special classes for the more intelligent, and a curriculum designed to give them at once a broad mental outlook and what is necessary in the way of expert knowledge. There is a tendency to suppose that knowledge which is useful cannot give culture, and vice versa. I believe this to be a delusion. It is held that knowledge of the Peloponnesian War gives culture, whereas knowledge about the Russian Revolution is vulgar and reprehensible. Views of this sort are an obstacle, not only to the acquisition of useful knowledge, but also to sound culture, which should have a breadth and catholicity of which it is perpetually being robbed by pedants.)

(The education of the bureaucrat will be an education for a special type of citizenship. But it will not be a sound education so long as some knowledge has special prestige owing to its being traditional, while other departments of knowledge are thought un-important because they are not possessed by pedagogues. At the time of the Renaissance, the bulk of good literature was in Latin or Greek; now, this is not the case. Most English public school-masters have not yet discovered this fact, and the British Government still selects its Civil Servants largely for proficiency in the classics, although a knowledge of French and German would be both more useful and of more cultural value. The narrow-ness of the traditional conception of culture has a great deal to do with the disrepute into which culture has fallen with the general public. Genuine culture consists in being a citizen of the universe, not only of one or two arbitrary fragments of space-time; it helps men to understand human society as a whole, to estimate wisely the ends that communi-ties should pursue, and to see the present in its relation to past and future. Genuine culture is therefore of great value to those who are to wield power, to whom it is at least as useful as detailed information. The way to make men useful is to make them wise, and an essential part of wisdom is a comprehensive mind.)

CHAPTER VII

THE HERD IN EDUCATION

ONE of the most important factors in the formation of character is the influence of the herd upon the individual during childhood and youth. (Many failures of integration in personality result from the conflict between two different herds to both of which a child belongs, while others arise from conflicts between the herd and individual tastes. It should be an important consideration in education to secure that the influence of the herd is not excessive, and that its operations are beneficial rather than harmful.)

(Most young people are subject to the operation of two different kinds of herd, which may be called respectively the great herd and the small herd. The great herd is one composed not exclusively of young people, but of the whole society to which the child belongs. This is determined in the main by the child's home, except where there is a very definite conflict between home and school, as happens, for example, with the children of immigrants in the United States. During the time that a boy or girl spends at school, the great herd is, however, of less importance than the small herd consisting of school-fellows. Every collection of human beings in habitual close proximity develops a herd feeling, which is

shown in a certain instinctive uniformity of behaviour, and in hostility to any individual having
the same proximity but not felt as one of the group.
Every new boy at school has to submit to a certain
period during which he is regarded with unfriendly
suspicion by those who are already incorporated
in the school herd. If the boy is in no way peculiar,
he is presently accepted as one of the group, and
comes to act as the others act, to feel as they feel,
and to think as they think. If, on the other hand,
he is in any way unusual, one of two things may
happen: he may become the leader of the herd,
or he may remain a persecuted oddity. Some very
few, by combining unusual good-nature with eccentricity, may become licensed lunatics, like "mad
Shelley" at Eton.

Conventional men acquire, during their school
years, that quick and almost instinctive realization
of what is demanded in order to be a conventional
member of the herd, which is needed for common-
place respectability in later life. If a fellow-member
of a club does anything which is not entirely correct, a man will remember from his boyhood the
kind of treatment which was meted out to queer
boys; and, while modifying his behaviour to suit the
code of adult civilization, he will still keep it, in
its essential pattern, what it became in those early
years. This constitutes the really effective moral
code to which men are subjected. A man may do
things which are immoral; he may do things which

are illegal; he may be callous, or brutal, or, on a suitable occasion, rude; but he must not do any of those things for which his class will cold-shoulder him. What these things are depends, of course, upon the country and the age and the social class concerned. But in every country, in every age, and in every social class, there are such things. \

Fear of the herd is very deeply rooted in almost all men and women. And this fear is first implanted at school. It becomes, therefore, a matter of great importance in moral education that the things punished by the school herd shall be, as far as possible, undesirable things which it is within the boy's power to alter. But to secure this is extremely difficult. The natural code for a herd of boys is, as a rule, not a very exalted one. And among the things which they are most likely to punish are things which do not lie within the power of their victims. A boy who has a birth-mark on his face, or whose breath is offensive, is likely to endure agonies at school, and not one boy in a hundred will consider that he deserves any mercy. I do not think this is inevitable. I think it is possible to teach boys a more merciful attitude, but the matter is difficult, and school-masters who like what is called manliness are not likely to do much in this direction.

More serious, from a social, though not from an individual, point of view, is the case of those boys whose larger herd is in some way in opposition to the smaller herd of the school, such as Jews in a school composed mainly of Gentiles. Most Jews, even in the most liberal societies, have been subjected during boyhood to insults on account of their race, and these insults remain in their memory, colouring their whole outlook upon life and society. A boy may be taught at home to be proud of being a Jew: he may know with his intellect that Jewish civilization is older than that of most Western nations, and that the contribution of Jews has been, in proportion to their numbers, incomparably greater than that of Gentiles. Nevertheless, when he hears other boys shout "Sheeney!" or "Ike!" after him in tones of derision, he finds it difficult to remember that it is a fine thing to be a Jew; and if he does remember it, he remembers it defiantly. In this way a discord is planted in his soul between the standards of home and the standards of school. This discord is a cause of great nervous tension, and also of a profound instinctive fear. Apart from Jewish nationalism, there are two typical reactions to this situation: one that of the revolutionary, the other, that of the toady. We may take Karl Marx and Disraeli as two extreme examples of these reactions. The hatred which Karl Marx felt for the existing order it is likely he would not have felt if he had been a Gentile. But having too much intelligence to hate Gentiles as such, he transferred his hatred from Gentiles as a whole to capitalists. And since capitalists were, in fact, largely

91

hateful, he succeeded, by viewing them with the eyes of hatred, in inventing a largely true theory of their place in the social order. Disraeli, who was a Jew in race but a Christian in religion, met the situation in another way. He admired, with the profoundest sincerity, the splendours of aristocracy and the magnificence of monarchy. There, he felt in his bones, was stability. There was safety from persecution. There was immunity from pogroms. The same fear of the hostile herd which, in Karl Marx, turned to revolution, turned in Disraeli to protective imitation. With amazing skill he made himself one of the admired herd, rose to supremacy within it, became the leader of a proud aristocracy, and the favourite of his sovereign. The keynote of his life is contained in his exclamation when the House of Commons laughed down his maiden speech: "The time will come when you *shall* hear me!" How different is the attitude of the born aristocrat in the face of laughter is illustrated by the story of the elder Pitt, who once began a speech in the House with the words: "Sugar, Sir—," which caused a titter. Looking round, he repeated in louder tones: "Sugar, Sir—," and again there was a titter. A third time, with looks of wrath, and in a voice of thunder, he repeated: "Sugar, Sir—." And this time not the faintest titter was to be heard.

Many kinds of eminence, both good and bad, have been caused by the boy's desire to wipe out some shame which he had suffered in the face of the herd. Of this sort of thing bastards afford an illustration. Edmund, in *Lear*, sets forth the way in which his being illegitimate has made him hostile to conventional people. I dare say William the Conqueror would not have been stirred to such notable deeds if he had not wished to wipe out the stain of his birth.

So far we have been considering the effect of quite ordinary herds upon individuals who were abnormal either in character or in circumstance. But not infrequently there have been boyish herds of a more extreme sort, more vicious and more cruel than the herds to which most of us were accustomed in youth. Kropotkin, in his youth, was a member of the corps of pages, the aristocratic school in which boys specially favoured by the Czar were educated. His descriptions of the things that occurred in this school are interesting. He says, for example:

" . . . The first form did what they liked; and not farther back than the preceding winter one of their favourite games had been to assemble the 'green-horns' at night in a room, in their nightshirts, and to make them run round, like horses in a circus, while the *pages de chambre*, armed with thick india-rubber whips, standing some in the centre and the others on the outside, pitilessly whipped the boys. As a rule the 'circus' ended in an Oriental fashion, in an abominable way. The moral conceptions which prevailed at that time, and the foul talk

93

which went on in the school concerning what occurred at night after a circus, were such that the least said about them the better."

The influence of the school herd upon the character of remarkable men can hardly be over-estimated. Take, for example, Napoleon. Napoleon, in his youth, was at the aristocratic military college at Brienne, where almost all the other boys were rich and of the higher nobility. He was there as a result of a political concession which France had made to Corsica, in virtue of which a certain small number of Corsican youths were educated at Brienne free of charge. He was one of a large family, and his mother was poor. After he became Emperor, it was conveniently discovered that he was descended from an ancient Ghibelline family, but this was not known at the time. His clothes were plain and threadbare, while the other youths were in gorgeous raiment. He was a despised nobody, whom they viewed with haughty disdain. When the Revolution broke out, he sympathized with it, and one may suspect that an element in his sympathy was the thought of the humiliation which was being brought upon the comrades of his years at Brienne. But when he rose to be Emperor, a more exquisite and Arabian-Nights type of revenge became possible. The very men who had despised him could now be made to sue for the privilege of bowing down before him. Can it be doubted that the snobbery that marred his later years of power had

94

its source in the humiliations which he had suffered as a boy? His mother, who had not suffered the same humiliations, viewed his career with cynical detachment, and, against his wishes, insisted upon saving a large part of her salary in preparation for the day when his glories should be at an end.

There have been a few great men, mostly monarchs, who never suffered the pressure of the herd at all. (The most notable of these is Alexander the Great, who was not at any time one among a crowd of equals. Perhaps both his greatness and his faults were due in part to this fact. He was not held back from magnificent conceptions by any such modesty as is instilled into the new boy at school. Conceiving of himself as a conqueror, it seemed natural to conquer the whole world. Conceiving of himself as greater than all his contemporaries, it seemed natural to think of himself as a god. In his dealings with his friends, even those who were nearest to him, he showed no sign of recognizing their rights. His murders of Parmenio and Cleitus, taken in isolation, suggest the cruel tyrant, but they are psychologically explicable as due to the impatience of a man who had at no time been subjected to the herd.

(The above illustrations are designed to suggest that the school herd is one of the most important factors in determining character, especially when it conflicts with some individual or social characteristic in a boy of exceptional talents. The man

95

who wishes to found a good school must think more about the character of the herd which he is creating than about any other single element. If he himself is kindly and tolerant, but permits the school herd to be cruel and intolerant, the boys under his care will experience a painful environment in spite of his excellences. I think that in some modern schools the doctrine of non-interference is carried to a point where this sort of thing may easily occur. If the children are never interfered with by the adults, the bigger children are likely to establish a tyranny over the smaller ones, so that the liberty which is supposed to be the watchword of the school will exist only for an aristocracy of the physically strong. It is, however, extremely difficult to prevent the tyranny of older children by means of direct disciplinary measures. If the grown-ups exercise force in their dealings with the older children, the older children will, in turn, exercise force in their dealings with the smaller ones. The thing to be aimed at is to have as little pressure of the herd as possible, and as little dominance of physical strength as is compatible with juvenile human nature. While it is well for boys and girls to learn the lesson of social dealings with their contemporaries, it is not well for them to be subjected to too intense a herd pressure. Herd pressure is to be judged by two things: first, its intensity, and second, its direction. If it is very intense, it produces adults who are timid and conventional, except in a few rare instances. This is regrettable, however excellent may be the moral standards by which the herd is actuated. In *Tom Brown's School-days* there is a boy who is kicked for saying his prayers. This book had a great effect, and among my contemporaries I knew one who had been kicked at school for *not* saying his prayers. I regret to say that he remained through life a prominent atheist. Thus even this highly virtuous form of herd tyranny, when carried too far, becomes undesirable. Too much herd pressure interferes with individuality, and with the development of all such interests as are not common among average healthy boys, e.g. science and art, literature and history, and every-thing else that makes civilization. It cannot be denied, however, that emulation within the herd has its good points. It encourages physical prowess, and it discourages all kinds of sneaking underhand meanness. Within limits, therefore, it has its uses.

These uses are much greater where the purposes of the herd are, on the whole, good, than where they are, for example, such as in Kropotkin's account of the "corps of pages." One of the advantages of special schools for boys and girls of unusual ability is that, in such schools, the herd is likely to be far more enlightened than in ordinary schools, and far less hostile to civilized pursuits. But even where completely ordinary boys and girls are concerned, it is possible, by means of grown-up example, to produce a certain degree of toleration and kindliness, and a considerable degree of interest in collective enterprises such as plays, for example, in which the herd instinct works co-operatively and not oppressively.

For certain exceptionally strong characters, there is an educational value in standing out against the herd for some reason profoundly felt to be important. Such action strengthens the will, and teaches a man self-reliance. Provided he is not made to suffer too much, this may be all for the good; but if the herd makes him unhappy beyond a point, he will either yield and lose what was most excellent in his character, or become filled with a destructive rage, which may, as in Napoleon's case, do untold harm to the world.

With regard to the larger herd that lies outside the school, parents whose opinions are in any way unconventional are faced with a perplexity which many of them find it very difficult to resolve. If they send their children to a school where unusual opinions are encouraged, or where unusual freedoms are permitted, they fear that, on entering the larger world, the boy or girl will not be readily adaptable to things as they are. Those who have been allowed to think and speak freely about sex will be oppressed by the usual reticences and pruderies. Those who have not been taught patriotism will have a difficulty in finding a niche in our nationalistic world. Those who have not been taught respect for constituted authority will find themselves in trouble through the freedom of their criticisms. And, in a word, those who have been used to freedom will feel the chains of slavery more irksome than those who have been slaves from birth. Such, at least, is the argument which I have frequently heard advanced by liberal-minded parents in favour of an illiberal education for their children.

(There are, I think, two answers to this argument, one comparatively superficial, the other fundamental. The first of these answers consists in pointing out that external conformity of behaviour is a thing which young people learn easily, and that, in fact, it is universally taught in all conventional systems of education, where the behaviour of children before parents and teachers is totally different from their behaviour with each other. It is, I believe, quite as easy to learn this conformity in adolescence as to learn it at an earlier age. To some degree it is a mere matter of good manners. It would be rude to talk to a Mussulman against Mahomet, or to a judge against the criminal law. It may be our public duty to express opinions on either of these subjects publicly, but it can hardly be our duty to express them privately in quarters where they can only cause pain and anger. I do not believe that a free education need make a boy or girl incapable of kindly manners, nor of that degree of external decorum which conventional life demands. Nor do I believe that the pain of conformity after a free education is nearly so great as the pain caused by

99

the complexes which are implanted in the course of a conventional education. So much for the first answer.

The second answer goes deeper. Our world contains grave evils, which can be remedied if men wish to remedy them. Those who are aware of these evils and fight against them are likely, it is true, to have less everyday happiness than those who acquiesce in the *status quo*. But in place of everyday happiness they will have something which I, for my part, value more highly, both for myself and for my children. They will have the sense of doing what lies in their power to make the world less painful. They will have a more just standard of values than is possible for the easy-going conformist. They will have the knowledge that they are among those who prevent the human race from sinking into stagnation or despair. This is something better than slothful contentment, and if a free education promotes this, parents ought not to shrink from the incidental pains which it may involve for their children.

CHAPTER VIII

RELIGION IN EDUCATION

RELIGION is a complex phenomenon, having both an individual and a social aspect. At the beginning of historical times, religion was already old: throughout history, increase of civilization has been correlated with decrease of religiosity. The earliest religions of which we know were social rather than individual: there were powerful spirits who punished or rewarded the whole tribe according as individual members of the tribe behaved offensively or pleasantly. The feelings of the spirits, as to the sort of behaviour that was offensive or pleasant, were ascertained by induction and recorded in priestly tradition. If an earthquake or a pestilence destroyed the inhabitants of some region, prudent men would enquire which of their habits were peculiar, and decide that such habits were in future to be avoided. This point of view is by no means extinct. I knew a Vicar in the Church of England who thought that the defeat of the Germans in the Great War was due to their fondness for the Higher Criticism, since he held that the Creator of the universe objects to textual exegesis of Hebrew manuscripts. (Religion, as its advocates are in the habit of telling us, is the source of the sense of social obligation. When a man did something displeasing to the gods, they were apt to punish not only the guilty individual but the whole tribe. Consequently his conduct was a matter of general concern, since private vices caused public calamities. This point of view still dominates the criminal law. There are sexual abnormalities for which men suffer imprisonment, although, from a rational standpoint, their behaviour concerns only themselves; if any justification of their punishment is to be attempted, it must be based upon what befell the Cities of the Plain, since only so can their conduct make any difference to the community. It is a curious fact that the things to which the gods object are seldom things that would do much harm if they did not arouse the divine wrath. They object to one's eating pork or eating beef or marrying one's deceased wife's sister; in the time of King David, God objected to a census, and slew so many people by a pestilence that King David's statistics were rendered worthless. The Aztecs' gods insisted on human sacrifice and cannibalism before they would show favour to their worshippers. Nevertheless, although the moral codes resulting from religion have been curious, it must be admitted that it is religion that has given rise to them. If any morality is better than none, then religion has been a force for good.

Although religion began as an affair of the tribe, it early developed also a purely individual aspect. From about the sixth century B.C., widely separated movements began in the ancient world, which concerned themselves with the individual soul and with what a Christian would call salvation. Taoism in China, Buddhism in India, the Orphic religion in Greece, and the Hebrew prophets, all had this character: they arose from the perception that the natural life is sorrowful, and from the search for a way of life which should enable men to escape misfortune, or at least to bear it. At a not much later date Parmenides inaugurated the great tradition of religious philosophy by his doctrine of the unreality of time and the one-ness of all things. From him as ancestor come Plato, Plotinus, the Fathers, Spinoza, Hegel, Bergson, and all the philosophers of mysticism. From the Hebrew prophets comes the type of religion which is concerned less with metaphysics than with righteousness; this type is predominant in Protestantism. In every form of Christianity there is both a moral and a metaphysical element, owing to the fact that Christianity arose from an intimate blend of Judaism and Hellenism; but on the whole, as Christianity travelled westward, it became less metaphysical and more moral. Islam, except in Persia, has always had only a very slight element of metaphysics, while the religions emanating from India have been predominantly philosophic.

(Ever since the rise of individual religion, the personal and the institutional elements in the religious life have been at war with one another. The institutional elements have usually been politically the stronger, since they were supported by priests and endowments and traditions, as well as by government and the law. Personal religion is a private matter, which should in no way concern the community. But institutional religion is a matter of great political importance. Wherever institutional religion exists, property is connected with it, and a man can make a living by advocating its tenets, but not (or not so easily) by opposing them. In so far as education is influenced by religion, it is influenced by institutional religion, which controls ancient foundations, and in many countries controls the State. At present, in most of the countries of Western Europe, religion dominates the education of the rich, while it has less influence on the education of the poor. This is to some extent a political accident: where no one religion is strong enough to impose itself on the State, State schools cannot teach the doctrines of a particular sect, but schools supported by the fees of the pupils can teach whatever parents think worth paying for. In England and France, largely as a result of this state of affairs, the rich are much more religious than the urban poor. When I say they are "religious," I am using the word in a political sense: I do not mean that they are pious, nor even necessarily that they give a metaphysical assent to Christian dogma, but only that they support the Church, vote with it in legislative questions, and wish their children to be in the care of those who accept its teaching.

It is for this reason that the Church is still important.

Among liberal-minded laymen, one meets, not infrequently, the view that the Church has ceased to be a weighty factor in the life of the community. This is, to my mind, a profound error. The law of marriage and divorce, though not quite what most ecclesiastics would wish, retains absurdities and cruelties—such as the refusal of divorce for insanity —which would not survive a week but for the influence of Christian Churches. Open opponents of Christianity are handicapped in many ways in competition with those who are more pious or more discreet; in practice, many posts are not open to avowed atheists, who require more ability to achieve success than is required by the orthodox.

It is in education, more than anywhere else, that institutional religion is important at the present day. In England, all public schools and almost all preparatory schools are either Anglican or Roman Catholic. It is sometimes said, by free-thinking parents who send their children to such schools, that most people react against their education, and that therefore it is as well to teach falsehood to the young in order that, after they have reacted, they may believe what is true. This argument is a mere excuse for timid conventionality, which a moment's reflection shows to be statistically fallacious. The immense majority of adults believe through life most of what they were taught in youth. Countries remain Protestant, Catholic, Mahometan, or whatever they may be, for centuries on end, whereas if the doctrine of reaction were true they ought to change their religion in each generation. The very men who advance such an argument for having their children taught orthodoxy show, by their conduct, how little they have reacted. If you believe privately that two and two are four, but avoid proclaiming this opinion, and hold it right that public money should be spent in teaching your children and the children of others that two and two are five, your effective opinion, from a social point of view, is that two and two are five, and your private personal conviction to the contrary becomes unimportant. So those who, while not themselves religious, believe a religious education to be desirable, have not in any effective way reacted against their own religious education, however they may protest to the contrary.

Many of those who do not give an intellectual assent to the dogmas of religion, hold that religion, nevertheless, is harmless and perhaps even beneficent. On this point I find myself at one with the orthodox, as opposed to what are called "liberal" thinkers: it seems to me that the questions whether there is a God and whether we persist after death are important, and that it is well to think as truly as possible on these matters. I cannot take the politician's view that, even if there be not a God, it is desirable that most people should think there is,

106

since this belief encourages virtuous conduct. Where children are concerned, many freethinkers adopt this attitude: how can you teach children to be good, they ask, if you do not teach them religion? How can you teach them to be good, I should reply, if you habitually and deliberately lie to them on a subject of the greatest importance? And how can any conduct which is genuinely desirable need false beliefs as its motive? If there are no valid arguments for what you consider "good" conduct, your conception of goodness must be at fault. And in any case it is parental authority rather than religion that influences the behaviour of children. What religion mainly does is to give them certain emotions, not very closely bound up with action, and not, for the most part, very desirable. Indirectly, no doubt, these emotions have effects upon behaviour, though by no means such effects as religious educators profess to desire. This, however, is a subject to which I shall return later.

The bad effects of religious education depend partly upon the particular doctrines taught and partly upon the mere insistence that various doubtful propositions are known to be true. Whether these propositions are in fact true or not may be undiscoverable, but in attempting to make the young regard them as certain, religious teachers are teaching what is false, since, whether true in fact or not, the propositions in question are emphatically not certain. Take, for example, the future life. On this matter wise men confess their ignorance: the evidence is insufficient, and suspense of judgement is the only rational attitude. But the Christian religion has pronounced in favour of a future life, and the young who are brought up under its influence are taught to regard survival after death as a certainty. "What does it matter?" the reader may say; "the belief is comforting, and cannot do any harm." I should reply that it does harm in the following ways.

First: any exceptionally intelligent child, who discovers by reflection that the arguments for immortality are inconclusive, will be discouraged by his teachers, perhaps even punished; and other children who show any inclination to think likewise will be discouraged from conversation on such topics, and if possible prevented from reading books that might increase their knowledge and their reasoning power.

Secondly: since most people whose intelligence is much above the average are nowadays openly or secretly agnostic, the teachers in a school which insists on religion must be either stupid or hypocritical, unless they belong to that small class of men who, owing to some kink, have intellectual ability without intellectual judgement. What happens in practice is that men who intend to adopt the scholastic profession begin at an early age to close their minds against adventurous thoughts; they become timid and conventional, first in theology and then, by a natural transition, in everything else; like the fox who had lost his tail, they tell their pupils that it is good to be timid and conventional; after they have done this for a sufficient length of time, their merit is observed by the authorities, and they are promoted to positions of power. The type of man who can keep his job as a teacher and make a success of his career is thus largely determined by the theological or other tests which, explicitly or implicitly, limit the choice of teachers, and exclude from the teaching profession most of those who are best fitted to stimulate the young both intellectually and morally.

(Thirdly: it is impossible to instil the scientific spirit into the young so long as any propositions are regarded as sacrosanct and not open to question. It is of the essence of the scientific attitude that it demands evidence for whatever is to be believed, and that it follows the evidence regardless of the direction in which it leads. As soon as there is a creed to be maintained, it is necessary to surround it with emotions and taboos, to state in tones vibrant with manly pathos that it contains "great" truths, and to set up criteria of truth other than those of science, more especially the feelings of the heart and the moral certainties of "good" men. In the great days of religion, when men believed, as Thomas Aquinas did, that pure reason could demonstrate the fundamental propositions of Christian theology, sentiment was unnecessary: St. Thomas's *Summa* is

109

as cool and rational as David Hume. But those
days are past, and the modern theologian allows
himself to use words charged with emotion so as
to produce in his reader a state of mind in which
the logical cogency of an argument will not be too
closely scrutinized. The intrusion of emotion and
sentimentality is always the mark of a bad case.
Imagine the methods of religious apologists applied
to the proposition $2 + 2 = 4$. The result would be
something as follows: "This great truth is acknow-
ledged alike by the busy man of affairs in his office,
by the statesman engaged in the computation of
the national revenue, by the booking-office clerk
in his efforts to meet the claims of the so-called
'rush hour,' by the innocent child buying lollipops
to delight his baby brother, and by the humble
Eskimo counting his catch of fish on the frozen
shores of the Arctic ocean. Can so wide a unani-
mity have been produced by anything other than
a deep human recognition of a profound spiritual
need? Shall we listen to the sneering sceptic who
would rob us of the shining heritage of wisdom
handed down to us from times less out of touch
with the infinite than our age of jazz? No! A thousand times No!" But it may be doubted whether
boys would learn arithmetic better by this method
than by those in vogue at present.

For such reasons as we have been considering,
any creed, no matter what, is likely to be harmful
in education when it is regarded as exempt from

the intellectual scrutiny to which our more scientific beliefs are subjected. There are, however, various special objections to the kind of religious instruction to which, in Christian countries, a large percentage of children are exposed.

In the first place, religion is a conservative force, and preserves much of what was bad in the past. The Romans offered human sacrifices to the gods as late as the second Punic War, but apart from religion they would not have done anything so barbaric. Similarly in our own day men do things from religious motives which, apart from religion, would seem intolerably cruel. The Roman Catholic Church still believes in hell. The Anglican Church, as a result of a decision of the lay members of the Privy Council against the opposition of the Archbishops of Canterbury and York, does not regard hell as *de fide*; nevertheless, most Anglican clergymen still believe in hell. All who believe in hell must regard vindictive punishment as permissible, and therefore have a theoretical justification for cruel methods in education and the treatment of criminals. The immense majority of ministers of religion support war whenever it occurs,[1] though in peace-time they are often pacifists; in supporting war, they give emphatic utterance to their conviction that God is on their side, and lend religious support to the persecution of men who think wholesale slaughter unwise. While slavery existed,

[1] On this subject, see quotations in Joad, *Under the Fifth Rib*, pp. 69 ff.

religious arguments were found in support of it; nowadays, similar arguments are found in support of capitalistic exploitation. Almost all traditional cruelties and injustices have been supported by organized religion until the moral sense of the lay community compelled a change of front.

In the second place, the Christian religion offers comforts to those who accept it, which it is painful to have to forgo when belief fades. Belief in God and a future life makes it possible to go through life with less of stoic courage than is needed by sceptics. A great many young people lose faith in these dogmas at an age at which despair is easy, and thus have to face a much more intense unhappiness than that which falls to the lot of those who have never had a religious upbringing. Christianity offers reasons for not fearing death or the universe, and in so doing it fails to teach adequately the virtue of courage. The craving for religious faith being largely an outcome of fear, the advocates of faith tend to think that certain kinds of fear are not to be deprecated. In this, to my mind, they are gravely mistaken. To allow oneself to entertain pleasant beliefs as a means of avoiding fear is not to live in the best way. In so far as religion makes its appeal to fear, it is lowering to human dignity.

In the third place, when religion is taken seriously, it involves viewing this world as unimportant in comparison with the next, thereby leading to the advocacy of practices which cause a balance of

112

misery here below on the ground that they will
lead to happiness in heaven. The chief illustration
of this point of view is in questions of sex, which
I shall consider in the next chapter. But there is
undoubtedly, in those who accept Christian teaching genuinely and profoundly, a tendency to mini-
mize such evils as poverty and disease, on the
ground that they belong only to this earthly life.
This doctrine falls in very conveniently with the
interests of the rich, and is perhaps one of the reasons
why most of the leading plutocrats are deeply
religious. If there is a future life, and if heaven is
the reward for misery here below, we do right to
obstruct all amelioration of terrestrial conditions,
and we must admire the unselfishness of those captains of industry who allow others to monopolize
the profitable brief sorrow on earth. But if the
belief in a hereafter is mistaken, we shall have
thrown away the substance for the shadow, and
shall be as unfortunate as those who invest a life-
time's savings in enterprises that go bankrupt.
(In the fourth place, the effect of religious teaching upon morality is bad in various ways. It tends
to sap self-reliance, especially when it is associated
with the confessional; through teaching the young
to lean upon authority, it often makes them incapable of self-direction. I have known men who
had been educated as Roman Catholics and who,
when they lost their faith, behaved in ways which
must be regarded as regrettable. Some would say

H   113

that such men show the moral utility of religion, but I should say quite the opposite, since the weakness of will which they display is a direct result of their education. Moreover, when religion is presented as the only ground for morality, a man who ceases to believe in religion is likely to cease to believe in morality. Samuel Butler's hero in *The Way of all Flesh* raped the housemaid as soon as he ceased to be a Christian. There are many sound reasons for not raping housemaids, but the young man in question had not been taught any of them; he had only been taught that such acts are displeasing to God. In view of the fact that, in our day, loss of faith is a quite probable occurrence, it is imprudent to base all morality, even the indispensable minimum, upon a foundation so likely to give way.

Another morally undesirable aspect of religious education is that it underestimates the intellectual virtues. Intellectual impartiality, a most important quality, it regards as positively bad; persistent attempts to understand difficult matters it views, at best, with toleration. The individuals whom it holds up for admiration in the present day are seldom men of first-rate intelligence; when they are, it is because of some folly to which they have given utterance in a foolish moment. Owing to the identification of religion with virtue, together with the fact that the most religious men are not the most intelligent, a religious education gives courage

to the stupid to resist the authority of educated men,
as has happened, for example, where the teaching
of evolution has been made illegal. So far as I can
remember, there is not one word in the Gospels in
praise of intelligence; and in this respect ministers .
of religion follow gospel authority more closely than
in some others. This must be reckoned as a serious
defect in the ethics taught in Christian educational
establishments.

The fundamental defect of Christian ethics consists in the fact that it labels certain classes of acts
"sins" and others "virtues" on grounds that have
nothing to do with their social consequences. An
ethic not derived from superstition must decide first
upon the kind of social effects which it desires to
achieve and the kind which it desires to avoid. It
must then decide, as far as our knowledge permits,
what acts will promote the desired consequences;
these acts it will praise, while those having a contrary tendency it will condemn. Primitive ethics
do not proceed in this way. They select certain
modes of behaviour for censure, for reasons which
are lost in anthropological obscurity. On the whole,
among successful nations, the acts condemned tend
to be harmful, and the acts praised tend to be
beneficial, but this is never the case as regards every
detail. There are those who hold that originally
animals were domesticated for religious reasons, not
from utility, but that the tribes which tried to
domesticate the crocodile or the lion died out,

while those which chose sheep and cows prospered. Similarly, where tribes with different ethical codes conflicted, those whose code was least absurd might be expected to be victorious. But no code with a superstitious origin can fail to contain absurdities. Such absurdities are to be found in the Christian code, though less now than formerly. The prohibition of work on Sunday can be defended rationally, but the prohibition of play and amusement cannot. The prohibition of theft is, in general, sound, but not when it is applied, as it was by the Churches in post-war Germany, to prevent public appropriation of the property of exiled princes. The superstitious origin of Christian ethics is most evident in the matter of sex; but this is so large a subject that it demands a separate chapter.

CHAPTER IX

SEX IN EDUCATION

THE opinions entertained by civilized adults on the subject of sex morals are not infrequently quite different from those which they desire to be taught to their children. There is a traditional moral code still accepted in all sincerity by a section of the population, but accepted by others only nominally and as a matter of respectability. In general, those whose opinions on sex matters are traditional have much more confidence in proclaiming and preaching their doctrines than have those who view the traditional code with doubt. Those who are prepared, in their own private behaviour and in their opinion of the private behaviour of their friends, to be latitudinarian, are seldom quite clear as to what their ethic is, and still more seldom willing to express publicly any dissent from the conventional code. Moreover, they tend to think that the strength of the sexual passion is sure to lead men and women into acts contrary to whatever code they may hold, and that therefore the right degree of liberty in action is most likely to be secured when theory is more stringent than a strict regard for truth would warrant. A person who thinks that in no circumstances whatever is sexual intercourse outside marriage justifiable may come, under the stress of deep love, to feel that in this particular case the circumstances are so peculiar as to allow of relaxation of the code. The person who thinks that a great love justifies relations outside marriage will tend to suppose that every passing fancy is a great love. The man who thinks that even passing fancies are legitimate, provided they are mutual and not mercenary, may be tempted to forget the mutuality and to introduce mercenary considerations surreptitiously. In such ways most people tend to a greater freedom in action than in theory. Therefore, in advocating any kind of sex freedom, it is always necessary to remember that the freedom which will be taken is likely to exceed that which is advocated.

Whatever view may be taken as to the right sexual morals for adults, there are a number of questions concerning the sex education of children which can be considered on grounds of common sense and psychology without raising any fundamental issues. It is the custom to leave education in the hands of persons exceptionally ignorant, bigoted, and narrow-minded. The children of the well-to-do are left, during their first years, very largely in the hands of nurses who are usually celibate and almost always prudish. When later they come under the care of more educated women, these women are still as a rule celibate, and it is expected that they should be of impeccable moral character. This means that as a rule they are timid, sentimental, and afraid of reality. It means also that their opinions on sex are

118

vehement, but ill-informed. School-masters, while not necessarily celibate, are expected to have a high moral tone, viz. to decide practical questions by traditional prejudice rather than by scientific psychology. Most of them would think the psychology of infantile sex a nasty subject, concerning which it is well to be ignorant. Of the harmful consequences of their ignorance they remain blissfully unaware.

Most children, by the time they are two years old, have already been taught to regard their sexual parts superstitiously as in some way mysterious and awful, and requiring to be treated in a quite special way. They are taught to mention their natural necessities in a whisper or by a euphemism, and if they are seen touching those parts of their anatomy which nurses consider intangible, they are severely lectured. I know men and women whose mothers saw them thus engaged when they were little children, and told them they would rather see them dead. (This is by no means uncommon.) I regret to say that they have not turned out patterns of conventional virtue. Masturbation is nearly universal among very young children, and is usually met with dire threats. In Germany, as one learns from Freud, boys are told that a stork\will come and mutilate them, and if by any chance they see a girl naked, they are likely to think that she is one to whom this has happened. Facts of this sort are well known to readers of psycho-analytic literature, but it is illegal for such literature to be read by those who are likely to do harm owing to not having read it. Nervous disorders in later life are frequently traceable to threats as to the consequence of masturbation by which infants are terrified. Throughout their school life boys are apt to be told by school-masters that masturbation leads to insanity. The truth is that the threats as to the evil consequences of masturbation not infrequently lead to insanity, but masturbation itself, so long as it is completely ignored by adults, does very little harm, especially in infancy.

The secrecy as to the method by which children come into the world has many bad effects. In the first place, it involves the belief that some knowledge is bad, and more especially that interesting knowledge is bad. It should be one of the fundamental principles of any sound ethic that all knowledge is good, and that to this no exception whatever can be admitted. The child who finds that his natural curiosity in certain directions is met with frowns and rebuffs learns to suppose that knowledge is good when it is uninteresting, but bad when it is interesting. In this way scientific curiosity becomes opposed to virtue, and the child's efforts to be good become efforts to be stupid, too often, alas! successful. For girls it is very bad to be kept in ignorance of the facts of gestation. Girls tend to feel themselves inferior to boys, and to wish that they were boys. So long as they do not know about gestation it appears as though men were better than women at almost everything. I have seen girls acquire a new respect for their sex, and a new contentment in being girls, as soon as they came to know of the part played by women in creating children. But if children are told the part of the mother without being told the part of the father, there is an unfairness to boys analogous to that which complete silence involves towards girls. Moreover, children who are fond of their fathers are glad to know that they have a physical connection with them as well as with their mothers. It is as necessary to the self-respect of boys to know the father's part in procreation as it is to that of girls to know the mother's part in gestation.

Another bad effect of the policy of silence about the facts of sex is that it causes children to know that their parents lie to them. Children generally find out the truth much sooner than parents suppose, and after they have found it out they not infrequently continue to ask questions of their parents, and register the untruthful answers with a certain youthful cynicism. Lying to children, although moralists do not think so, is an undesirable practice, and an ethic which demands it can hardly be sound.

It is important that information on sexual subjects should be given in exactly the same tone of voice, and in the same manner, as information on other subjects. And it should be given with the same directness. There is a certain school of thought which considers that children should first be told about the loves of flowers, then about the innocent gambols of lobsters, and only after a long biological preface about the behaviour of their own parents, which by this time they will think requires a very elaborate apology. It is only inhibited adults who feel that this long preface is necessary. To the child, if he is not corrupted by the prudery of his elders, sex seems a perfectly natural subject just like any other. If parents are unable themselves to speak naturally on this subject, they should have their children spoken to by someone less cramped by convention and inhibition. Before puberty there is no difficulty whatever in causing a child to remain natural about sex, and to view it exactly as he views other subjects. This is the ideal to be aimed at throughout life, but after puberty it becomes more difficult of attainment. But the difficulty, even after adolescence, will be very much less when children have been brought up sanely than when their minds have been filled with irrational terrors and taboos.

The problems which arise with older boys and girls are difficult to treat apart from some positive sexual ethic. The usual view is that complete continence should be aimed at, and cannot do any harm. In England, all hetero-sexual experience is prevented by segregation of the sexes, except in the case of a few unusually enterprising youths. There is consequently a tendency among the more enterprising to homosexuality, and among the more

122

timid to masturbation. Boys are told, and many of them believe, that these practices are wicked and harmful. They have to be furtive, since if discovered they are visited by severe punishment. Discovery is, of course, largely a matter of accident, and therefore punishment falls in an unjustly capricious way. But the fear of punishment and the practice of conceal-ment have of necessity a bad effect upon those who remain undetected. In public schools there is a tendency to sacrifice intelligence to virtue by keep-ing the boys so busy and so tired physically that they will have neither leisure nor inclination for sex. The existing system thus has the following disadvantages: first, it plants superstitious terrors in the minds of boys; secondly, it causes a large percentage to become timid hypocrites; thirdly, it makes thought and feeling on sexual subjects obscene and sur-reptitious; fourthly, it causes scientific curiosity to appear sinful, so that it either decays or becomes morbid; fifthly, it leads to the discouragement of leisure, and therefore of intellectual growth.

In spite of these evils of the present system, it is not easy, short of a complete change in the whole moral code, to imagine any system free from grave objections. From puberty to marriage is, with most men in the modern community, a considerable stretch of years. Even assuming it to be desirable that they should spend these years in complete con-tinence, it is certain that most men will not do so. Yet so long as the present moral code persist, they

can hardly infringe it without some damage. To go
with prostitutes is a bad thing, first on account of
the danger of disease, secondly, because prostitution
is an undesirable profession, at any rate so long as
prostitutes are looked down upon, thirdly, because
if a man's first experiences of sex are mercenary and
devoid of all sentiment, he is likely when he comes
to marriage to view his wife either as a prostitute or
as a saint, neither of which is likely to lead to
happiness. Masturbation after puberty, while it does
not do as much harm as conventional moralists
pretend, undoubtedly has certain grave evils. It
tends to make a man self-centred and unadven-
turous, and sometimes it makes him incapable of
normal intercourse. It is possible that homosexual
relations with other boys would not be very harmful
if they were tolerated, but even then there is the
danger lest they should interfere with the growth of
normal sexual life later on. If the sexes are not
segregated, there is likely to be a good deal of intercourse between girls and boys, which will not only
interfere gravely with education, but will cause
pregnancies at an age when they are undesirable.
I do not think that in the present state of society and
public opinion there is any solution to this problem.
Perhaps a time will come when the psychological
disorders caused in adolescence by our present code
will be taken so seriously that boys and girls will be
allowed the kind of freedom at present allowed in
Samoa and various other Pacific islands. If this ever

comes to be a practice, it will be necessary to give instruction in contraception, and to interrupt pregnancies at once if they nevertheless occur. I cannot say that I like such a prospect, and perhaps it may be found that continence during the years of adolescence would impose no intolerable burden if there were a prospect that the necessity for it would cease at about the age of twenty. This could be secured by Judge Lindsey's system of companionate marriage. I am sure that university life would be better, both intellectually and morally, if most university students had temporary childless marriages. This would afford a solution of the sexual urge neither restless nor surreptitious, neither mercenary nor casual, and of such a nature that it need not take up time which ought to be given to work.

Before puberty the question of sex in education can be treated on lines of mental hygiene without the necessity of forming any very definite judgement on sexual ethics. But it is difficult to decide how sex should be treated in the later years of school and at the university unless we have fairly clear opinions as to what we think desirable and what undesirable in sexual behaviour. The sexual ethic of most people at the present time is a confused jumble derived from three main sources: first, the insistence upon the virtue of wives which is necessary for the institution of the patriarchal family; second, the Christian doctrine that all sex outside marriage is sin; and third, the entirely modern doctrine of the equality of women: Of these three elements, that derived from the patriarchal family is the oldest. It can be seen at the present day in Japan without the other two. The Japanese are very free from all sex taboos, and their sexual morality contains little that is superstitious. There is no pretence of sex equality, and women are kept strictly subordinate to men. The patriarchal family is very firmly established, and is enforced by the subjection of wives rather than abstract moral teaching. Young children are allowed sexual knowledge, sexual conversation, and sexual play to a degree which is astonishing to a European. The morality of adult life is one applying only to women, and imposed upon them ruthlessly by the superior power of men. This is an ancient system which was nearly universal in pre-Christian civilizations.

Early Christianity introduced the belief that there is something inherently impure about sex, so that it can only be excused by the necessity of propagating the human race, and even when confined to marriage is scarcely so honourable as continence. I do not mean to say that no such feeling existed before the rise of Christianity: there is some element in human nature which makes men prone to anti-sexual feelings, and it was to these already existing elements that Christianity appealed. The Jews had had strong sexual taboos, but had not had any feeling of the impurity of sex as such, though traces of the rise of this feeling are to be found in the

126

Apocrypha. The Christian ethic, for the first time in history, was theoretically equal as between men and women, although in practice departures from virtue were regarded more leniently in the case of men than in the case of women. Christian practice thus came to be not so very different from that of pre-Christian patriarchal civilizations, though there remained a great psychological difference in the fact that men's sexual freedoms were regarded as sins.

With the advent of the doctrine of sex equality, this system broke down. Either men must become as virtuous as women, as the pioneers of feminism hoped, or women must be allowed to be as unvirtuous as men, as the feminists of our generation tend to urge. But if virtue is not demanded of women, it is difficult to see how the patriarchal family can be maintained, and to abandon the patriarchal family would involve profound changes in the social structure. There is thus a confusion. Christian ethics have always been too severe for male human nature, and if women are to be as free as men they also will find Christian ethics intolerably severe. The family is a very deeply rooted institution, which men will not willingly see transformed. From this confusion there seems only one clear issue, which is that the place of the father should be taken by the State—a system which is easily possible under Communism, but not so easy to adapt to the institutions of private property and inheritance. In this way the question of private property becomes bound up with the question of sexual morals. It cannot be expected that a man will work to support children who may not be his, and therefore the system of private property, combined with the patriarchal family, involves a certain degree of virtue in wives. To demand virtue of wives, but not of husbands, is contrary to the doctrine of sex equality, and it is difficult to see how virtue is to be secured without either tyranny or taboo. I have little doubt that the solution will be found in the greatly diminishing importance of the father and an increasing tendency for children to be supported by the State rather than by their fathers. I am not at all sure that this will be a good thing. The sentiment of paternity, and the feeling of sons towards their fathers, have been profoundly important elements in the history of civilization, and I do not profess to know what civilization will be like without these elements. But whether for good or evil, the importance of the State in relation to children seems bound to increase, while the importance of the father will correspondingly diminish.

Of all these modern problems and confusions, those who are concerned with the education of the young refuse to take any notice. They hold that the rigid Christian ethic, even if it cannot be enforced upon adults, can and should govern the attitude of those who have the care of the young. The moral attitude of schools and of British Universities remains much more rigid than that of the world at large, with the result that education becomes increasingly out of touch with the society for which it is supposed to be preparing young people. While public opinion and social institutions remain what they are, I do not think that any clear-cut solution is possible, because of the fundamental incompatibility between sex equality and the patriarchal family. In spite of this incompatibility, however, a good deal can be decided by general ethical principles, and by the refusal to treat sex in a superstitious manner.

⊦ It should be an absolute principle in all dealings with the young not to tell them edifying lies. It should be an absolute principle that every subject is open to rational debate, and to consideration in a scientific manner. If the preservation of the patriarchal family is to be the basis of morals, it is difficult to see how from this basis to deduce the sinfulness of such sexual practices as cannot lead to offspring, although it is these, more than any others, that are viewed with horror, not only by Christian ethics, but also by the criminal law. It should be realized also that even when a certain kind of conduct is in itself desirable, it may not be desirable to enforce it by a very rigid discipline, or by the creation of morbid terrors. These principles cover a considerable part of the moral education of the young. For the rest, I think we must wait until our chaotic and rapidly changing society has developed into some more stable form.

It is important in all dealings with the young to prevent them from acquiring the notion that sex is something inherently nasty and furtive. Sex is an interesting subject, and it is natural to human beings to think and talk about it. At present, this entirely natural desire on the part of the young is treated by the authorities as something wicked, with the result that the young acquire even more interest in the subject than they would naturally have, and converse about it continually with all the pleasure of forbidden fruit. Their conversation is necessarily ignorant and foolish, because they are left to their own guesses and their own half-knowledge. The whole subject of sex becomes to most boys a matter of sniggering[1] and dirty stories. The whole conception of sex as a matter of natural delight, rising on occasion to poetry, sometimes light-hearted and gay, sometimes passionate with a tragic profundity, lies outside the purview of the pedagogic moralists, to whom sex is wicked when it is combined with delight, and virtuous only when it is drab and habitual. Poetry and joy and beauty are thrust out of life by this morality of ugliness, and something stark and rigid is brought into all human relationships. From this outlook come prudery and petty-mindedness and the death of imagination. It may be that a freer outlook also has its dangers. But they are the dangers of life, not of death.

CHAPTER X

PATRIOTISM IN EDUCATION

EVERY man has a number of purposes and desires,
some purely personal, others of a sort which he can
share with many other men. Most men desire
money, for example, and most ways of growing
rich involve co-operation with some group. The
group concerned depends upon the particular way
of growing rich. For most purposes, two different
firms in the same business are rivals, but for purposes
of a protective tariff they co-operate. Money, of
course, is not the only thing for which people fall
into groups of a political kind. They are organized
into churches, brotherhoods, learned societies, free-
masons, and what not. The motives which lead men
to co-operate are many :(identity of interest is one;(
identity of opinion is another; and ties of blood are)
yet a third. The Rothschild family co-operated
owing to ties of blood. They did not need formal
articles of incorporation, because they could trust
each other, and a great part of their success was due
to the fact that there was a Rothschild in every
important financial centre in Europe. A form of
co-operation based upon identity of opinion is to be
seen in the philanthropic work of the Quakers after
the war. They were able to work together easily
because of their similarity of outlook. Ties of self-

interest are the basis of such organizations as joint-stock companies and trade-unions.

A group of men organized for a purpose has collectively only that purpose for the sake of which the organization exists. Its mentality is therefore simpler and cruder than that of any individual. The Society for Psychical Research, let us say, cares only for psychical research, though each of its members cares for many other things. The Federation of British Industries cares only about British industries, although its individual members may enjoy going to the play or watching a cricket match. A family as a whole cares only about the family fortunes, and is frequently willing to sacrifice individual members to this end.

(Passions which are politically organized are much more powerful than those which remain unorganized. The people who wish to go to cinemas on Sundays are a totally unorganized crowd, and are politically of little account. The Sabbatarians who wish them not to go are organized, and have political influence. The cinema proprietors also are organized. From a political point of view, therefore, the question of the Sunday opening of cinemas is a conflict between cinema proprietors and Sabbatarians, in which the wishes of the general public do not count.

A given man may belong to a number of organizations, some useful, some harmful, some merely innocent. He belongs, let us say, to the British

Fascists, to the football club in his village, and to a society for anthropological research. In the third capacity he is laudable, in the second innocent, and in the first abominable. He himself is a mixture of good and bad, but the organizations have an unmixed ethical character for good or evil which is not to be found in their members. It is the purpose for which men are organized which determines' whether an organization is good or bad, not the character of the men composing the organization.

These somewhat trite remarks are intended to lead up to the curious results which flow from the organization of men into States. In almost all civilized countries, the State is the most powerful of the organizations to which a man belongs, so that his purposes *qua* member of a State are much more effective politically than any of his other purposes. It becomes important, therefore, to consider what the purposes of the modern State are.

The functions of the State are partly internal, partly external. For this purpose I include local government among the functions of a State. One may say, broadly speaking, that the internal purposes of the State are good, while its external purposes are bad. This statement is, of course, too simple to be literally true, but it represents a useful first approximation. The internal purposes of the State include such matters as roads, lighting, education, the police, the law, the post-office, and so on. One may quarrel with this or that detail of administration, but only an anarchist will hold that such purposes are in themselves undesirable. (So far as its internal activities are concerned, therefore, the State, on the whole, deserves the loyalty and support of its citizens.)

When we come to its external purposes the matter is otherwise. (In relation to the rest of the world, the purposes of a great State are two: defence against aggression, and the support of its citizens in foreign exploitation. Defence against aggression, in so far as it is genuine and needed to prevent invasion, may be allowed to be *prima facie* useful. But the difficulty is that the very same means which are required to prevent invasion are also convenient for foreign exploitation. The leading States of the world aim at drawing an economic tribute from the labour and the mineral wealth of less powerful countries, and employ in securing this tribute the armed forces of which the nominal purpose is defensive. When, for example, the Transvaal was found to contain gold, the British invaded it. Lord Salisbury assured the nation that "we seek no goldfields." But somehow or other we happened to go where goldfields were, and to find ourselves in possession of them at the end of the war. To take another illustration: everybody knows that the British went to Southern Persia from a desire to benefit the Southern Persians, but it is doubtful whether we should have taken so much interest in their welfare if they had not inhabited a country full of oil. Not dissimilar re-

marks might be made about some of the doings
of the United States in Central America. In like
manner, the motives of Japan in going to Man-
churia are, of course, the noblest possible; but they
happen, by some curious accident, to coincide with
the interests of the Japanese.)

It is not too much to say that most of the external
activities of powerful States in the present day are
concerned with the employment, or the threat, of
armed forces, for the purpose of taking away from
the less powerful wealth which legally belongs to
them. Activities of this sort on the part of private
individuals are considered criminal, and are punished by law unless they are on a very large scale.
But on the part of nations, they are considered
admirable by the citizens of the nations concerned.

This brings me at last to the subject of the present
chapter, namely, the teaching of patriotism in
schools. (In order to judge of this teaching it is
necessary to be clear not only as to its intentions,
but also as to its actual effects. Patriotism, in intention, and in the thoughts of those who advocate it,
is a thing which is very largely good. Love of home,
love of one's native country, even a certain degree
of pride in its historical achievements, in so far as
these are deserving of pride, is not to be deprecated.
It is a complex sentiment, partly concerned with
actual love of the soil and of familiar surroundings,
partly with something analogous to an extended
love of family. The root of the sentiment is partly

135

geographical and partly biological. But this primitive feeling is not in itself either political or economic. It is a feeling for one's own country, not against other countries. In its primitive form it is hardly to be found except among those who live in rural surroundings without much travel. The town-dweller who is perpetually changing his habitation, and has no piece of land that he can call his own, has much less of the primitive sentiment out of which patriotism grows than has the rural land-owner or peasant. The town-dweller has, instead, a sentiment largely artificial, largely the product of his education and his newspapers, and almost wholly harmful. This sentiment is not so much love of home and of compatriots as hatred of foreigners and desire to appropriate foreign countries. Like almost all bad sentiments, it is disguised as loyalty. If you wish a man to commit some abominable crime, from which he would naturally recoil in horror, you first teach him loyalty to a gang of arch-criminals, and then make his crime appear to him as exemplifying the virtue of loyalty. Of this process, patriotism is the most perfect instance. Take, for example, reverence for the flag. The flag is the symbol for the nation in its martial capacity. It suggests battle, war, conquest, and deeds of heroism. The British flag suggests to a Briton Nelson and Trafalgar, not Shakespeare or Newton or Darwin. Things which have been done by Englishmen to further the civilization of mankind have not

136

been done under the symbol of the flag, and are not called to mind when that symbol is venerated. The best deeds of Englishmen have been done by them not as Englishmen, but as individuals. The deeds which Englishmen do with the consciousness of being Englishmen, and because they are Englishmen, are of a less admirable sort. But it is these deeds that the flag calls upon us to admire. And what is true of the British flag is equally true of the Stars and Stripes, or of the flag of any powerful nation.

Throughout the Western world boys and girls are taught that (their most important social loyalty is to the State of which they are citizens, and that their duty to the State is to act as its government may direct. Lest they should question this doctrine, they are taught false history, false politics, false economics. They are informed of the misdeeds of foreign States, but not of the misdeeds of their own State. They are led to suppose that all the wars in which their own State has engaged are wars of defence, while the wars of foreign States are wars of aggression. They are taught to believe that when, contrary to expectation, their own country does conquer some foreign country, it does so in order to spread civilization, or the light of the gospel, or a lofty moral tone, or prohibition, or something else which is equally noble. They are taught to believe that foreign nations have no moral standards, and, as the British national anthem asserts, that it is the duty of Providence to "frustrate their knavish tricks"—a duty in which Providence will not disdain to employ us as its instruments. The fact is that every nation, in its dealings with every other, commits as many crimes as its armed forces render possible. Citizens, even decent citizens, give a full assent to the activities which make these crimes possible, because they do not know what is being done, or see the facts in a true perspective.)

For this willingness of the ordinary citizen to become an unconscious accomplice in murder for the sake of robbery, education is chiefly to blame. There are those who blame the Press, but in this I think they are mistaken. The Press is such as the public demands, and the public demands bad newspapers because it has been badly educated. Patriotism of the nationalistic type, so far from being taught in schools, ought to be mentioned as a form of mass-hysteria to which men are unfortunately liable, and against which they need to be fortified both intellectually and morally. (Nationalism is undoubtedly the most dangerous vice of our time—far more dangerous than drunkenness, or drugs, or commercial dishonesty, or any of the other vices against which a conventional moral education is directed. All who are capable of a survey of the modern world are aware that, owing to nationalism, the continuance of a civilized way of life is in jeopardy. This, I say, is generally known to all persons who are well-informed as to international affairs. Nevertheless, everywhere public money continues to be spent in propagating and intensifying this destructive vice. Those who consider that children should not be taught to regard wholesale slaughter as the noblest work of man are denounced as renegades, and friends of every country but their own. One would have supposed that natural affection would cause many people to feel pain in the thought of their children dying in agony. Such is not the case. Although the danger is patent, all attempts to cope with it are viewed as wicked by most of the holders of power in most countries. Military service is represented as a noble preparation for the defence of one's own country, and not a word is said to make young people aware that the military operations of their own country, supposing it to be a powerful one, are much more likely to consist of foreign aggression than of home defence.

The objections to patriotic teaching are various. \There is the objection which we have already considered that, unless the virulence of nationalism can be abated, civilization cannot continue. There is the objection that it is hardly possible to teach civilized human ideals of conduct in an institution which also teaches people how to kill. There is the objection that the teaching of hatred, which is a necessary part of a nationalistic education, is in itself a bad thing. But over and above all these, there is the purely intellectual objection that the ' teaching of nationalism involves the teaching of false propositions.) In every country of the world,

139

children are taught that their country is the best, and in every country except one this proposition is false.] Since the nations cannot agree as to which is the one where it is true, it would be better to give up the habit of emphasizing the merits of one nation at the expense of every other. The idea that what is taught to children should, if possible, be true is, I know, very subversive, and in some of its applications even illegal. But I cannot resist the conviction that instruction is better when it teaches truth than when it teaches falsehood. History ought to be taught in exactly the same way in all countries of the world, and history text-books ought to be drawn up by the League of Nations, with an assistant from the United States, and another from Soviet Russia. History should be world history rather than national history, and should emphasize matters of cultural importance rather than wars. In so far as wars must be taught, they should not be taught only from the point of view of the victor, and of heroic deeds. The pupil should linger on the battle-field among the wounded, should be made to feel the plight of the homeless in devastated regions, and should be made aware of all the cruelties and injustices for which war affords an opportunity. At present almost all the teaching is of a sort to glorify war. Against the teaching of the schools, the labours of pacifists are vain. This, of course, applies especially to schools for the rich, which are everywhere morally and intellectually inferior to schools for the poor. Children learn in school the faults of other nations, but not the faults of their own. To know the faults of other nations ministers only to self-righteousness and war-like feeling, whereas to know the faults of one's own nation is salutary. What English boy is taught in school the truth about the Black and Tans in Ireland? What French boy is taught the truth about the occupation of the Ruhr by coloured troops? What American boy is taught the facts about Sacco and Vanzetti, or Mooney and Billings? Owing to such omissions, the ordinary citizen of every civilized country is wrapped in self-complacency. He knows about other nations all the things they do not know about themselves; but the things they know about his country, he does not know.

Most of the teaching of patriotism, while intellectually misguided, is morally innocent. The men who teach have themselves been taught on a wrong system, and have learned to feel that, in a world where foreigners are so wicked, only great military efforts can preserve their own country from disaster. There is, however, a less innocent side to patriotic propaganda. There are interests which make money out of it, not only armament interests, but also those who have investments in what are called undeveloped countries. If you possess, let us say, oil in some rather unsettled country, the expense of getting the oil consists of two parts—first, the technical, straight-forward expense of extracting it, and second, the political or military expense of keeping the "natives" in order. Only the former part of the expense falls upon you; the second part of the expense, which may be much greater, falls upon the tax-payer, who is induced to undertake it by means of patriotic propaganda. In this way, a highly undesirable connection grows up between patriotism and finance. This again is a fact which the young are carefully prevented from knowing.

Patriotism in its more militant forms is intimately bound up with money. The armed forces of the State can be, and are, employed for the enrichment of its citizens. This is done partly by exacting tribute or indemnities, partly by insisting upon the payment of debts which would otherwise be repudiated, partly by the seizure of raw materials, and partly by means of compulsory commercial treaties. If the whole process were not covered by the glamour of patriotism, its sordidness and wickedness would be evident to all sane people. Education could easily, if men chose, produce a sense of the solidarity of the human race, and of the importance of international co-operation. Within a generation, the vehement nationalism from which the world is suffering could be extinguished. Within a generation, the tariff walls by which we are all making ourselves poor could be lowered, the armaments with which we are threatening ourselves with death could be abolished, and the spite with which we are cutting off our own noses could be replaced by goodwill. The nationalism which is now everywhere rampant mainly a product of the schools, and if it is to be rought to an end, a different spirit must pervade ducation.

This matter, like disarmament, will have to be lealt with by international agreement. Perhaps the League of Nations, if it can spare any time from the vhitewashing of aggressors, may sooner or later recome aware of the importance of this matter. Perhaps the governments may agree to a uniform reaching of history. Perhaps after the next great war, the survivors, if any, may come together and decide to substitute the flag of the League of Nations for their several national flags. But no doubt these are Utopian dreams. It is the nature of teachers to teach what they know, however little that may be. Imagine English teachers of history threatened by an international agreement with the necessity of teaching world history. They would have to find out the date of the Hegira and when Constantinople fell. They would have to learn about Jenghiz Khan and Ivan the Terrible, about how the mariner's compass spread from China to the Arab sailors, and how the Greeks were the first to make statues of the Buddha. Their indignation at having such demands made upon their time would know no bounds, and they would agitate for a new government pledged to flout the League of Nations. The active energy of our time throughout the Western world is in capitalist enterprise, and is, on the whole, a force making for destruction. The classes of men who should make for something better, such as teachers, are for the most part fairly content with the *status quo*. Any social amelioration would involve a change in their lessons, and has on that account to be avoided if possible. The effort that they wish to avoid is not only intellectual, but also emotional. Familiar emotions come easily, and it is difficult to teach oneself to feel new emotions on a familiar occasion, such as the playing of the national anthem. And thus our modern world, where the good are lazy and only the bad are energetic, goes reeling drunkenly towards destruction. At moments men see the abyss, but the intoxication of unreal sentiments soon closes their eyes. To all who are not intoxicated, the danger is clear. And nationalism is the chief force impelling our civilization to its doom.

NOTE.—The present situation as regards nationalism in State schools in England is illustrated by the recent dismissal of Miss Beryl Aylward from her position as teacher at Coventry because she refused to salute the flag on Empire Day. She stated that, being a Quaker, she held the glorification of one's own country to be not conducive to international good will. It appears, therefore, that no conscientious Quaker or pacifist can hold a post as teacher in an English State school.

CHAPTER XI

CLASS-FEELING IN EDUCATION

EVER since the dawn of civilization, class inequality
has existed. Among savage tribes at the present day,
it takes very simple forms. There are chiefs, and the
chiefs are able to have several wives. Savages, unlike
civilized men, have found a way of making wives a
source of wealth, so that the more wives a man has
the wealthier he becomes. But this primitive form of
social inequality soon gave way to others more
complex. In the main, social inequality has been
bound up with inheritance, and therefore, in all
patriarchal societies, with descent in the male line.
Originally, the greater wealth of certain persons was
due to military prowess. The successful fighter acquired wealth, and transmitted it to his sons. Wealth
acquired by the sword usually consisted of land, and
to this day land-owning is the mark of the aristocrat, the aristocrat being in theory the descendant
of some feudal baron, who acquired his lands by
killing the previous occupant and holding his
acquisition against all comers. This is considered
the most honourable source of wealth. There are
others slightly less honourable, exemplified by those
who, while completely idle themselves, have acquired their wealth by inheritance from an indus-
trious ancestor; and yet others, still less respectable,

whose wealth is due to their own industry. In the modern world, the plutocrat who, though rich, still works, is gradually ousting the aristocrat, whose income was in theory derived solely from ownership of land and natural monopolies. There have been two main legal sources of property: one, the aristocratic source, namely, ownership of land; the other, the bourgeois source, namely, the right to the produce of one's own labour. The right to the produce of one's own labour has always existed only on paper because things are made out of other things, and the man who supplies the raw material exacts right to the finished product in return for wage or, where slavery exists, in return for the bare necessaries of life. We have thus three orders men—the land-owner, the capitalist, and the proletarian. The capitalist in origin is merely a man whose savings have enabled him to buy the raw materials and the tools required in manufacturing and who has thereby acquired the right to the finished product in return for wages. The three categories of land-owner, capitalist, and proletarian are clear enough in theory; but in practice the distinctions are blurred. A land-owner may employ business methods in developing a seaside resort which happens to be upon his property. A capitalist whose money is derived from manufacture may invest the whole or part of his fortune in land, and take living upon rent. A proletarian, in so far as he money in the savings bank, or a house which he buying on the instalment plan, becomes to that extent a capitalist or a land-owner as the case may be. The eminent barrister who charges a thousand guineas for a brief should, in strict economics, be classified as a proletarian. But he would be indignant if this were done, and has the mentality of a plutocrat.

From a practical point of view, the important class distinctions outside the U.S.S.R. depend upon the patriarchal family and the practice of inheritance. Owing to the patriarchal family, the children of the rich get a different education, though not always a better one, than is given to the children of the poor. Owing to inheritance, the children of the rich may look forward, if they so desire, to idleness without starvation. If there were no such thing as inheritance, the inequalities of wealth which would survive would be obliterated in each generation. And if there were no such thing as the patriarchal family, the children of the rich would not be educated differently from the children of the poor. Socialists are apt to speak of the capitalist system in a somewhat vague way, without an adequate analysis of the different factors which contribute to it. The business activities of the capitalist are by no means the whole of the capitalist system. The fact that his children are in a privileged position owing to his wealth is an essential part of it. I do not mean this as a criticism of Marxism, since Marx realized the connection between economics and the family.

But I do say it in criticism of a good many English-speaking Socialists, who imagine that the economic structure of society has no very vital connection with marriage and the family. As a matter of fact, the connection is reciprocal. The bourgeois who is concerned in amassing private property applies the conception of private property to his wife and children, and has in consequence a certain way of feeling in regard to them. Conversely, sexual jealousy and paternal affection are emotions leading men to desire private property in women and children. And from their desire for this form of private property they are led to desire other forms also. In a primitive community, a man may desire wealth in order to have many wives. In a civilized community, one of the reasons for desiring wealth is to be able to give a better social status to one's wife and children than belongs to the wives and children of wage-earners. The connection of private property in material things with private property in women and children is thus reciprocal. It cannot be expected that one will break down without the other also breaking down. Private property in women and children introduces rivalry in regard to them, and thus brings the motive of class distinction into education. How all these matters would be affected by a thoroughgoing communism I do not propose to consider at this stage.

Where education is concerned it is, of course, the social position of the fathers that determines that of

148

the children. Thus in any society in which class distinctions exist, children are respected not solely on account of their own merits, but also on account of the wealth of their fathers. The children of the rich acquire a belief that they are superior to the children of the poor, and an attempt is made to cause the children of the poor to think themselves inferior to the children of the rich. It is necessary to make this effort with the children of the poor, since otherwise they might come to resent the injustice of which they are the victims. Consequently, wherever class distinctions exist, education necessarily has two correlative defects: that of producing arrogance in the rich, and that of aiming at irrational humility in the poor. The objections to the arrogance of the rich are obvious, and have been pointed out by the moralists from the time of the Hebrew prophets downwards, though only a small percentage of the moralists have noticed that the evil could not be undone by mere preaching, but only by a different economic system. The evils of attempting to produce irrational humility in the poor are somewhat different. If it is produced, initiative and self-respect are harmfully diminished. If it is not produced, there is resentment tending to destructiveness. Whether it is produced or whether it is not, the attempt to produce it involves the teaching of falsehood: ethical falsehood, since it is a representation that the inequality of the rich and the poor is not an injustice; economic falsehood, since it is suggested

149

that the present economic system is the best possible; historical falsehood, since the previous conflicts of rich and poor are narrated from the standpoint of the rich. When the teachers are little better than proletarians themselves, they need slavish souls if they are to believe what they have to teach, and lack of courage if they are to teach it without believing it.\

(In pre-industrial societies, where wealth is mainly aristocratic, the defence of inequality takes the form of reverence for birth, which often overrides the reverence for actual wealth, and conceals the economic origin of the sentiment. A penniless exiled chieftain may be more respected than a successful money-lender. Nevertheless, fundamentally it is wealth that is respected, because as a rule in such societies it is aristocratic descent which is the source of wealth. Where aristocracy is strong, belief in it is, of course, bolstered up by all kinds of nonsense, such as that aristocrats have better manners, more education, or finer feelings than other people. In a plutocratic society, such as that of the United States, there is a different form of humbug. The successful plutocrat is supposed to have achieved his position by hard work, frugality, and scrupulous honesty. He is supposed to use his position as a public trust, with an eye always to the general good. In the sixties and seventies of the last century, when the great fortunes of plutocrats were a novelty, traditional culture, such as that of the Adams family, exposed with gusto the tricks and chicanery and sheer illegality by which many of the leading men had amassed their wealth.[1] Throughout the eighties and nineties, books were written against the methods of the Standard Oil Company. Nowadays, this is all changed. The great plutocrats are regarded as great public benefactors. Every university has, or hopes to have, endowments from them. Every young man of academic tastes hopes to receive a research fellowship from the bounty of some philanthropic billionaire. The universities and the press are filled with the praise of the very rich, and the man in the street is taught to believe that virtue is proportional to income. Class distinctions are thus just as important in a country like the United States as they are in an aristocratic country, and a good deal more important than they are in countries such as Norway and Denmark, where there is- diffused comfort with hardly any great fortunes.

The harm done by class distinctions is not confined to the children. It extends to the teachers and the curriculum. More social prestige attaches to care of the mind than to care of the body, and therefore the teacher who gives intellectual instruction is usually indifferent to questions of health, and ignorant of the signs by which the first approaches of any physical ailment can be detected. The distinction between mind and body is artificial and

[1] See *High Finance in the Sixties*, by the Brothers Adams. Reprinted by the Yale University Press.

unreal; but unfortunately it has had an effect upon the social hierarchy, with the result that care of the body and care of the mind are much more separated in education than they ought to be. This, of course, is nothing like as bad as it was in former days, when a deaf child might be punished for inattention for years on end without any of the teachers discovering that he was deaf. But although such extreme instances as this are not likely to occur nowadays, the evil still exists in less flagrant forms. The teacher, for example, knows nothing about the child's digestive condition, and may be indignant at stupidity and bad temper for which the cause is to be found in constipation. If it were suggested to teachers that they should pay any attention to the bowel action of their pupils, their snobbery would be outraged. I do not wish the reader to misunderstand me at this point. I am not denying that in all modern schools there is physical care of children, and that a great deal is done to keep them in health, as compared with what used to be done in former times. What I am complaining of is that physical and mental care are so completely separated, and that the person who possesses the knowledge required for the one has, as a rule, no inkling of the knowledge required for the other. In an adult there is a considerable gulf between mind and body, but this gulf has no metaphysical necessity. It is a product of education. In a baby there is no gulf, in an infant there is very little, and in a child not much.

I do not suppose that a child of ten could give a very good philosophical account of the difference between mind and body. But every child would understand at once if you said: "Your mind is what is looked after by Miss A., and your body is what is looked after by Miss B." It is the distinction between Miss A. and Miss B. that underlies the subsequent metaphysical distinction between mind and matter. If the functions of Miss A. and Miss B. were combined in a Miss C., all children would grow up to be neutral monists, believing that mind and matter are only different aspects of the same phenomenon. In this way, metaphysics is connected with the class system. Mental activity is that which does not involve the use of arms or legs. Physical activity is that which does. Mental activity is superior to physical, because those who practise it exclusively need servants to do their physical labours for them. It follows that the soul is nobler than the body, that matter is the evil principle, and so on.

As regards the curriculum also, respect for wealth has had an effect, though this effect is less obvious than formerly. The Greeks, like all communities that employ slave labour, held the view that all manual work is vulgar. This led them to place a great emphasis upon such things as culture and philosophy and rhetoric, which could be studied without the use of the hands. They tended to think that all manipulation of matter was unworthy of a gentleman, and this probably had something to do with their partial lack of success in experimental science. Plutarch, relating the ingenious inventions of Archimedes during the siege of Syracuse, defends him from the charge of vulgarity on the ground that he was doing it for the benefit of his cousin the King. The Romans inherited the Greek view of culture, and down to our own day this view has been dominant in all countries of Western Europe. Culture is something which can be acquired by reading books, or by conversation. Whatever involves more than this is not culture in the Greek meaning of the term. And the Greek meaning of the term is still that adopted, at any rate in England, by most schoolmasters, many university teachers, and all old gentlemen with literary tastes. This applies not only to Greek and Roman antiquity, but also to modern history. It is considered more cultured to know about Horace Walpole than about Henry Cavendish, about Bolingbroke than about Robert Boyle, though in each case the latter was the more important man. All this is ultimately connected with the idea that a gentleman is one who does not use his hands unless it be in the noble art of war. A gentleman may use a sword, but should not use a typewriter.

In matters of this sort, the United States is much ahead of Europe, owing to the fact that, in America, aristocracy was abolished with emphasis at a time when it still existed in every European country. But a new form of class distinction in education is

154

CLASS-FEELING IN EDUCATION

growing up, which is the distinction between business management and the technical processes of
manufacture. The man engaged in business management is the aristocrat of the future, and the phrase
"a great executive" has much the same connotations
in modern America that the phrase "a great nobleman" had in the novels of Disraeli. The substitution
of the great executive for the great nobleman as the
type to be admired is having a considerable effect
upon ideals of culture. A great nobleman, in the
dithyrambic day-dreams of Disraeli, was, no doubt,
a man possessed of power, but it was power which
had come to him without his having had to seek it,
and which he exercised somewhat lazily. He was
possessed also of great wealth, but this, again, had
come to him without exertion, and he affected to
think little of it. The things upon which he prided
himself were his exquisite manners, his knowledge
of good wine, his familiarity with the great world of
all civilized countries, his judgement in regard to
Renaissance pictures, and his capacity for epigram.
It may be said generally that the accomplishments
of aristocrats were frivolous, but innocent. The
accomplishments of the great executives of our own
time are very different. They are men whose position has been achieved by their powerful will, and
their capacity for judging other men. Power is their
ruling passion, organizing is the activity in which
they excel. They are men capable of doing the
greatest good or the greatest harm, men who must

be respected for their abilities and their importance, and loved or hated according to the nature of their work, but never viewed with indifference or condescension. In an industrial world men of this type must come to the fore. In the U.S.S.R. men of this type are utilized by the State in ways which give scope for their abilities, without permitting the ruthless individualism of which they are allowed to be guilty in the capitalist world. But whether under capitalism or under communism, it is men of this type who must ultimately dominate an industrial civilization, and the difference between their mentality and that of aristocrats of former times must have an important influence in making industrial culture different from that of feudal and commercial ages.

The conception of "the education of a gentleman" has had a bad effect upon universities. Young people who are not exceptionally intellectual find it difficult in the years between eighteen and twenty-two to take very seriously the acquisition of academic knowledge, which is going to be of no direct use to them in later life. They tend, therefore, to be idle at the university, or if they work, to do so from mere thoughtless conscientiousness. For those whose profession is going to be research, the universities are admirable, but for most of the rest they are too much out of touch with subsequent life. It is possible to spend the university years in the acquisition of knowledge which has some professional utility, but conservative academic types view this with horror. I think they are mistaken. I think many clever young men become vapid and cynical through the consciousness that their work has no real importance while they are at the university. This does not happen to those who are studying medicine or engineering or agriculture or any subject of which the utility is obvious. A gentleman is intended to be ornamental rather than useful, but in order to be adequately ornamental he has to be supplied with an unearned income. For those who will have to earn their living, it is hardly wise to attempt a form of education whose main purpose was to make idleness elegant. Pure learning as an ideal has its place in the life of the community, but only for those few who are going to devote their energies to research. For those who are going to be engaged in some other profession, it would be better to spend the last years of education in acquiring such knowledge as would enable them to pursue their profession with intelligence and breadth of outlook. There is no such thing nowadays as an all-round education, but there is a tendency, especially in England, to over-emphasize those elements in education which enable a man to talk with seeming intelligence. Moreover, knowledge acquired at the university, if it is quite unrelated to subsequent professional work, is likely to be soon forgotten. If professional men of forty were examined in the subjects that they had studied at the university, I am afraid it would be found that in most cases very little knowledge remained. Whereas, if they had studied something which enabled them to see their profession in relation to the life of the community, and to understand its social aspects, it is likely that their subsequent experiences would have supplied illustrations to what they had learned, and would therefore have caused the knowledge to remain in their minds.

I have dealt hitherto with incidental disadvantages derived from class-distinctions, but I have only touched upon the greatest disadvantage, which is ethical. Wherever unjust inequalities exist, a man who profits by them tends to protect himself from a sense of guilt by theories suggesting that he is some way better than those who are less fortunate. These theories involve a limitation of sympathy, and opposition to justice, and a tendency to defend the *status quo*. They thus make the more fortunate members of the community into opponents of all progress; fear invades their souls, and they shrink timidly from all doctrines that they suspect of having a subversive tendency, and of being therefore a threat to their own comfort. On the other hand, the less fortunate members of the community must either suffer such intellectual atrophy that they do not perceive the injustice of which they are the victims, and such moral loss of self-respect that they are willing to bow down before men intrinsically no better than themselves, or they must be filled with anger and resentment, protesting indignantly, feeling a continual sense of grievance, and gradually coming to view the world through the jaundiced eyes of the victim of persecution mania. All tolerated injustice has thus two bad sides: one as regards the fortunate, and the other as regards the unfortunate. It is for these reasons rather than from any abstract excellence in justice for its own sake that unjust social systems are evil. In a community based upon injustice, the ethical side of education can never be what it should be. Emotions of resentment which, considered in themselves, are bad, may be a very necessary motive force in eliminating injustice, whether between classes, nations, or sexes. But they do not cease to be intrinsically undesirable by being politically necessary. And it should be a touch-stone of the good society that, in it, the useful emotions will be those that are kindly, friendly, and constructive, rather than those that are angry and destructive. This consideration, if followed out, will lead us very far. But as our theme is education, I will leave it to the reader to carry the argument to its conclusion.)

CHAPTER XII

COMPETITION IN EDUCATION

OF the dominant ideals of the nineteenth century, some have survived into our age, and some have not. Those that have survived have, for the most part, a more restricted field of application in our day than they had a hundred years ago. And of these the ideal of competition is a good example. It is, I think, a mistake to regard the belief in competition as due to Darwinism. The opposite is really the case: it was Darwinism that was due to belief in competition. The modern biologist, while he still believes in evolution, has much less belief in competition as its motive force than Darwin had; and this change reflects the change which has come over the economic structure of society. Industrialism began with large numbers of small firms all competing against each other, and at first with very little help from the State, which was still agricultural and aristocratic. Early industrialists, therefore, believed in self-help, *laisser faire*, and competition. From industry, the idea of competition spread to other spheres. Darwin persuaded men that competition between different forms of life was the cause of evolutionary progress. Educationists became persuaded that competition in the class-room was the best way to promote industry among the scholars.

Belief in free competition was used by employers as an argument against trade-unionism, and is still so used in the backward parts of America. But competition between capitalists gradually diminished. The tendency has been for the whole of one industry to combine nationally, so that competition has become mainly between nations, and much less than formerly between different firms within a given nation. Meantime, it has naturally been the endeavour of capitalists, while combining themselves, to hinder combinations as much as they could where their employees were concerned. Their motto has been: "United we stand; divided they fall." Free competition has thus been preserved as a Great Ideal in all provinces of human life, except in the activities of industrial magnates. Where the industrial magnates are concerned, the competition is national, and therefore takes the form of encouraging patriotism.

In education, the ideal of competition has had two kinds of bad effects. On the one hand, it has led to the teaching of respect for competition as opposed to co-operation, especially in international affairs; and on the other hand, it has led to a vast system of competitiveness in the class-room, and in the endeavour to secure scholarships, and subsequently in the search for jobs. This last stage has been somewhat softened, where wage-earners are concerned, by trade-unionism. But among professional men it has retained all its unmitigated severity.

One of the worst defects of the belief in competition in education is that it has led, especially with the best pupils, to a great deal of over-education. At the present day there is a dangerous tendency, in every country of Western Europe, though not in North or South America, to inflict upon young people so much education as to be damaging to imagination and intellect, and even to physical health. Unfortunately, it is the cleverest of the young who suffer most from this tendency: in each generation the best brains and the best imaginations are immolated upon the altar of the Great God Competition. To one who has, as I have had, experience at the university of some of the best minds of a generation, the damage done by over-strain in youth is heart-rending. The educational machine in the United States is in many ways inferior to those of Western Europe, but in this respect it is better than they are. Able young post-graduates in America seldom have the breadth of culture or the sheer extent of erudition that is to be found in the same class in Europe, but they have a love of knowledge, an enthusiasm for research, and a freshness of intellectual initiative which in Europe have usually given place to a bored and cynical correctness. To learn without ceasing to love learning is difficult, and of this difficulty European educators have not found the solution.

The first thing the average educator sets to work to kill in the young is imagination. Imagination is lawless, undisciplined, individual, and neither correct nor incorrect; in all these respects it is inconvenient to the teacher, especially when competition requires a rigid order of merit. The problem of the right treatment of imagination is rendered more difficult by the fact that, in most children, it decays spontaneously as interest in the real world increases. Adults in whom imagination remains strong are those who have retained from childhood something of its emancipation from fact; but if adult imagination is to be valuable, its emancipation from fact must not spring from ignorance, but from a certain lack of slavishness. Farinata degli Uberti held Hell in great contempt, in spite of having to live there for ever. It is this attitude towards fact that is most likely to promote fruitful imagination in the adult.

To pass to more concrete considerations, take such a matter as children's drawing and painting. Most children, from about five years old to about eight, show considerable imagination of a pictorial kind if they are encouraged but otherwise left free. Some, though only a small minority, are capable of retaining the impulse to paint after they have become self-critical. But if they have been taught to copy carefully and to aim at accurate representation, they become increasingly scientific rather than artistic, and their painting ceases to show any imagination. If this is to be avoided, they must not be shown how to draw correctly except when they themselves ask for instruction, and they must not be allowed to think that correctness constitutes merit. This is difficult for the teacher, since artistic excellence is a matter of opinion and individual taste, whereas accuracy is capable of objective tests. The social element in school education, the fact of being one of a class, tends, unless the teacher is very exceptional, to lead to emphasis upon socially verifiable excellences rather than upon such as depend upon personal quality. If personal quality is to be preserved, definite teaching must be reduced to a minimum, and criticism must never be carried to such lengths as to produce timidity in self-expression. But these maxims are not likely to lead to work that will be pleasing to an inspector.

The same thing, at a slightly later age, applies to the teaching of literature. Teachers tend to teach too much, and to make up silly rules of style, such as that no sentence should begin with "and" or "but." Definite rules of grammar must of course be observed, though even grammar is more elastic than most teachers suppose. Any child who wrote:

And damned be him that first cries hold, enough

would be reproached not only for profanity but also for bad grammar. In regard to literature, as in regard to painting, the danger is lest correctness should be substituted for artistic excellence. The teaching of literature should be confined to reading, and the reading should be intensive rather than extensive. It is good to know by heart things from

164

which one derives spontaneous pleasure, and it is totally useless, from the standpoint of education in literature, to read anything, however classical, which does not give actual delight to the reader. The literature that is read with avidity and known intimately moulds diction and style, whereas the literature that is read once coldly merely promotes pseudo-intelligent conversation. Pupils should, of course, write as well as read, but what they write should not be criticized, nor should they be shown how, in the teacher's opinion, they might have written it better. So far as writing is concerned, there should be no teaching.

Passing from imagination to intellect, we find somewhat similar considerations relevant, together with certain others connected with fatigue. Fatigue may be general or special; the former is to be considered in connection with health, but the latter should be borne in mind by all who are engaged in intellectual training. Readers may remember Pavlov's dog, who learnt to distinguish ellipses from circles. But as Pavlov gradually made the ellipses more nearly circular, there came at last a point—where the ratio of major and minor axes was $9:8$ —at which the dog's powers of discrimination gave way, and after this he forgot all that he had previously learnt on the subject of circles and ellipses. The same sort of thing happens to many boys and girls in school. If they are compelled to tackle problems that are definitely beyond their powers, a kind

165

of bewildered terror seizes hold of them, not only in relation to the particular problem in question, but also as regards all intellectually neighbouring territory. Many people are bad at mathematical subjects all their lives because they started them too young. Of the capacities tested in school, the power of abstract reasoning is the latest to develop, as may be seen from the data collected in Piaget's valuable book on *Judgment and Reasoning in the Child*. A pedagogue, unless he is very psychological and very experienced, cannot believe that children are as muddle-headed as they are: so long as the right verbal responses are obtained, it is supposed that the subject is understood. Arithmetic and mathematics generally are learnt at too early an age, with the result that, in regard to them, many pupils acquire the artificial stupidity of Pavlov's canine student of geometry. To prevent this kind of misfortune, it is necessary that teachers should have some knowledge of psychology, considerable training in the art of teaching, and a certain freedom to relax the curriculum where necessary. To know how to teach is at present thought desirable in those who teach the poor, but the sons of "gentlemen" are still taught by wholly untrained teachers. This is one of the unpredictable results of snobbery.

Fatigue damages the actual quality of the intellect, and is therefore very grave. Less disastrous, though still seriously harmful, is the discouragement of interest in intellectual things which results from

166

the fact that much of what is taught is (or at least seems) wholly useless. Take any average class of a hundred boys: I should guess that ninety of them learn only from fear of punishment, nine from a competitive desire for success, and one from love of knowledge. This lamentable state of affairs is not inevitable. By means of short hours, voluntary lessons, and good teaching, it is possible to cause about 70 per cent. to learn from love of knowledge. When this motive can be invoked, attention becomes willing and unstrained, with the result that fatigue is greatly diminished and memory greatly improved. Moreover, the acquisition of knowledge comes to be felt as a pleasure, with the consequence that it is likely to be continued after the period of formal education is ended. It will be found that more is learnt in the shorter hours of voluntary lessons than in the longer times of enforced and inattentive boredom. But the teacher must adapt the instruction to the pupils' sense of what is worth knowing, and not attempt to bully them into an insincere pretence that ancient rubbish has some occult and mysterious value.

Another intellectual defect of almost all teaching, except the highest grade of university tuition, is that it encourages docility and the belief that definite answers are known on questions which are legitimate matters of debate. I remember an occasion when a number of us were discussing which was the best of Shakespeare's plays. Most of us were

167

concerned in advancing arguments for unconventional opinions, but a clever young man, who, from the elementary schools, had lately risen to the university, informed us, as a fact of which we were unaccountably ignorant, that *Hamlet* is the best of Shakespeare's plays. After this the subject was closed. Every clergyman in America knows why Rome fell: it was owing to the corruption of morals depicted by Juvenal and Petronius. The fact that morals became exemplary about two centuries before the fall of the Western Empire is unknown or ignored. English children are taught one view of the French Revolution, French children are taught another; neither is true, but in each case it would be highly imprudent to disagree with the teacher, and few feel any inclination to do so. Teachers ought to encourage intelligent disagreement on the part of their pupils, even urging them to read books having opinions opposed to those of the instructor. But this is seldom done, with the result that much education consists in the instilling of unfounded dogmas in place of a spirit of inquiry. This results, not necessarily from any fault in the teacher, but from a curriculum which demands too much apparent knowledge, with a consequent need of haste and undue definiteness.

The most serious aspect of over-education is its effect on health, especially mental health. This evil, as it exists in England, is a result of the hasty application of a Liberal watchword, "equality of opportunity." Until fairly recent times, education was a prerogative of the sons of the well-to-do, but under the influence of democracy it was felt, quite rightly, that higher education ought to be open to all who could profit by it, and that ability to profit by it depended in the main upon intellect. The solution was found in a vast system of scholarships depending upon scholastic proficiency at an early age, and to a very large extent upon competitive examinations. Belief in the sovereign virtues of competition prevented anyone from reflecting that boys and girls and adolescents ought not to be subjected to the very severe strain involved. If the strain were only intellectual it would be bad enough, but it is also emotional: the whole future of a boy or girl, not only economically, but socially, turns upon success in a brief test after long preparation. Consider the situation of an intelligent boy from a poor home, whose interests are almost wholly intellectual, but whose companions care nothing for books. If he succeeds in reaching the university, he may hope to make congenial friends and spend his life in congenial work; if not, he is doomed not only to poverty but to mental solitude. With this alternative before him, he is almost certain to work anxiously but not wisely, and to destroy his mental resiliency before his education is finished.

While the evil is obvious to every one who has experience of teaching in a university, the remedy is not easy to devise. It is probably undesirable, and

169

certainly financially impossible, to give a university education to everybody; consequently some method of selection is necessary, and the method must depend chiefly upon intellectual proficiency. It would be better if the strain were not so concentrated as it is when it depends upon an examination, and if teachers could select a certain proportion of their pupils on the basis of their general impression. No doubt this would lead to a certain amount of toadying and favouritism, but probably these evils would be less grave than those of the present system. It would be well to select those who were to have a university education at the age of twelve, after which they should not be subjected to competition, but only to reasonable conditions of industry. And at the age of twelve they should be selected rather for intelligence than for actual proficiency.

This is a merit in the intelligence tests, which are too little used in England, though in America they are relied upon to an extent for which there is, to my mind, no scientific justification. Their merit is not that they are infallible—no test can be that— but that they bring out more or less correct results on the whole, and that they do not demand the exhausting and nerve-racking preparation which is required for the usual type of examination.

In urban areas, and wherever there is a sufficient density of population, there ought to be special schools for very clever boys and girls, as there already are for the mentally deficient. A beginning has been made in this direction in America,[1] but as yet only on a small scale.

Some of the results are interesting. For example: a boy whose intelligence quotient was 190 (100 being the average) was found in an ordinary school, where he had no friends and was regarded as a fool. He was transferred to a special class for boys with median intelligence quotient 164, where he was quickly recognized as a leader and "was elected to many posts of trust and honour." A great deal of needless pain and friction would be saved to clever children if they were not compelled to associate intimately with stupid contemporaries. There is an idea that rubbing up against all and sundry in youth is a good preparation for life. This appears to me to be rubbish. No one, in later life, associates with all and sundry. Bookmakers are not obliged to live among clergymen, nor clergymen among book-makers. In later life a man's occupation and status give an indication of his interests and capacities. I have, in my day, lived in various different social strata—diplomatists, dons, pacifists, gaol-birds, and politicians—but nowhere have I found the higgledy-piggledy ruthlessness of a set of boys. Intellectual boys, for the most part, have not yet learnt to conceal their intellectuality, and are therefore exposed to constant persecution on account of their oddity. The more adaptable among them learn, in time, to seem ordinary and to put on a smooth and vacuous

[1] See *Gifted Children*, by Hollingworth, Chapters IX and X.

exterior, but I cannot see that this is a lesson worth learning. If you walk through a farmyard, you may observe cows and sheep and pigs and goats and geese and ducks and hens and pigeons, all behaving in their several ways: no one thinks that a duck should acquire social adaptability by learning to behave like a pig. Yet this is exactly what is thought so valuable for boys at school, where the pigs tend to be the aristocracy.

The advantages of special schools for the cleverer children are very great. Not only will they avoid social persecution, thereby escaping much pain and emotional fatigue and all the lessons in cowardice which cause clever adults often to prostitute their brains in the service of powerful fools. From a purely intellectual point of view they can be taught much faster, and not have to endure the boredom of hearing things that they already understand being explained to the other members of the class; moreover, their conversation with each other is likely to be of a sort to fix knowledge in their memory, and their spare-time occupations can be intelligent without fear of ridicule. Nothing can be urged against such schools except administrative difficulties and that form of democratic sentiment which has its source in envy. At present, every clever boy or girl feels odd; in such an environment this feeling would disappear.

. One of the difficulties of every large educational machine is that the administrators are, as a rule,

172

not teachers, and have not the experience required for knowing what is possible and what is impossible. When a man begins to teach, unless he teaches selected groups of specially intelligent pupils, he finds with surprise that young people learn much less and much more slowly than he had supposed. A subject may be well worth knowing, but nevertheless not worth teaching, because in the time available most pupils will learn nothing of it. The tendency of those who construct a curriculum without having experience of teaching is to put too much into it, with the result that nothing is learnt thoroughly. On the other hand, the experienced teacher is apt to have a different bias, which is just as undesirable : he tends, largely because he must place pupils in order of merit, to prefer those subjects in which there can be no doubt whether the pupil has given the right answer. The long vogue of Latin grammar has been partly attributable to this source. Arithmetic, for the same reason, is overvalued; in British elementary schools it takes up far more of the time than it should. The average man should be able to do accounts, but beyond that he will seldom have occasion for sums. What he may have learnt of complicated arithmetic will be of no more practical use to him in later life than would the amount of Latin he could have learnt in the same time, and of far less use than what he could have learnt of anatomy and physiology and elementary hygiene.

The problem of over-education is both important and difficult. It is important because a clever person who has been over-educated loses spontaneity, self-confidence, and health, and thereby becomes a far less useful member of the community than he might have been. It is difficult because, as the existing mass of knowledge grows greater, it becomes increasingly laborious to know all that is relevant, both in the more complicated practical questions and in scientific discovery. We cannot therefore avoid the evils of over-education by merely saying: "Let boys and girls run wild and not be bothered with too much learning." Our social structure increasingly depends upon trained and well-informed intelligence. The present world-wide depression is largely due to lack of education on the part of practical men: if bankers and politicians understood currency and credit, we should all, from the highest to the lowest, be much richer than we are. The advancement of science—to take another illustration —cannot continue at anything like its present rate unless a man can reach the frontiers of existing knowledge by the time he is twenty-five, since few men are capable of profound originality after the age of thirty. And the average citizen cannot play his part in a complicated world unless he is more accustomed than at present to view practical issues as matters to be decided by the application of trained intelligence to masses of fact, rather than by prejudice, emotion, and clap-trap. For all these

174

reasons, intellectual education is a vital necessity in the modern social order.

There must be sufficient instruction, and there must not be the evils of over-education. This demands three things. First and foremost, there must be as little emotional strain as possible in connection with the acquisition of knowledge; this requires great changes in the system of examinations and scholarships, and the segregation, wherever possible, of the cleverer pupils. Emotional strain is the chief cause of harmful fatigue; purely intellectual fatigue, like muscular fatigue, is repaired each night during sleep, but emotional fatigue prevents sufficient sleep or makes it unrestful through bad dreams. During education, therefore, young people should, as far as is at all possible, have a care-free existence.

The second thing required is a drastic elimination of instruction that serves no useful purpose. I do not mean that children and young people should only acquire what is termed "useful" knowledge, but that they should not learn things merely because they always have been learnt. I have frequently questioned young people lately finished with school as to what they had learnt of history. I have generally found that they had done English history from Hengest and Horsa to the Norman Conquest, over and over again, in each new class, and that beyond that they knew nothing. I may be exceptional, but I have never yet found myself in a situation where it was really profitable to know about (say) the

175

relations of the kingdoms of Mercia and Wessex in the eighth century. There is much in history that is abundantly worth knowing, but this is hardly ever taught in schools.

The third thing required is that all higher instruction should be given with a view to teaching the spirit and technique of inquiry rather than from the standpoint of imparting the right answers to questions. Here, again, examinations are to blame. The young person who has to pass (say) an elementary examination in English literature will probably be well advised to read no single word of any of the great writers, but to learn by heart some manual giving all the information except what is worth having. For the sake of examinations, young people have to learn by heart all kinds of things, such as dates, which it is far more sensible to look up in books of reference. The proper sort of instruction teaches the use of books, not useless feats of memory designed to make books unnecessary. This is already recognized as regards post-graduate work, but it ought to be recognized at a much earlier stage of education. And the pupil's research should not be judged by the orthodoxy or otherwise of the conclusion arrived at, but by the extent of knowledge and the reasonableness of the argument. This method will not only teach the power of forming sound judgements and keep alive the learner's initiative, but will make the acquisition of knowledge interesting, thereby diminishing very greatly

176

the amount of fatigue involved in the process. The fatigue of intellectual work is largely due to the effort of forcing oneself to give attention to what is boring, and therefore any method that removes the boredom also removes most of the fatigue.

By these methods it is possible to become highly educated without endangering health and spontaneity. But this is not possible while the tyranny of examinations and competition persists. Competition is not only bad as an educational fact, but also as an ideal to be held before the young. What the world now needs is not competition but organization and co-operation; all belief in the utility of competition has become an anachronism. And even if competition were useful, it is not in itself admirable, since the emotions with which it is connected are the emotions of hostility and ruthlessness. The conception of society as an organic whole is very difficult for those whose minds have been steeped in competitive ideas. Ethically, therefore, no less than economically, it is undesirable to teach the young to be competitive.

CHAPTER XIII

EDUCATION UNDER COMMUNISM

In previous chapters we have seen the evils produced in education by the institution of private
property and its connection with the patriarchal
family. We have now to consider whether, under
communism, other equally grave evils are to be
expected, or whether, on the contrary, public
education could be better under communism than
it can ever be under capitalism.

The present state of education in the U.S.S.R.,
while it must be considered in this connection, is of
course by no means decisive, since Russia is still
engaged in construction, and is still far from the
ultimate goal. It is more instructive, for our purpose,
to consider what the Soviet Government hopes and
intends than what it has already achieved. What has
been done hitherto is necessarily in the nature of a
compromise. At the outbreak of the Revolution a
majority of Russians were illiterate, and the peasants,
who formed 80 per cent. of the population, were
highly conservative in their mentality. Lack of
funds, lack of school buildings, lack of teachers,
have all been grave obstacles. In spite of all these
difficulties, enough has been done to make it
fairly clear what the educational system will be
when it is completed. We will therefore consider

first what is now being done in education and then attempt to appraise the intended educational future.

A more or less official account is given by Albert P. Pinkevitch, President of the Second State University of Moscow, in his book on *The New Education in the Soviet Republic*, published in London by Williams & Norgate, Ltd. This book may be accepted as authoritative on all questions as to the scholastic organization and its present purposes. Many readers may be surprised to find how much there is that is similar to what exists in Western countries. To teach children to read and write and do sums is a piece of technical work which is not very much affected by the economic system. Questions of health, also, are uncontroversial. But in addition to such matters it will be found that there are systems of boy scouts, of teaching school morale, of inculcating loyalty to the State, and so on, which are closely similar to those in use in England and America. And something of the familiar outlook of the University President, as known in the United States, pierces through the unfamiliar communist phraseology. In spite of these echoes of older systems, however, there is much that is new, and what is new is of great importance.

The intimate connection of education with the social system, which has been emphasized in the foregoing pages, is, of course, asserted almost too definitely by all communists. Pinkevitch quotes from

Lenin a passage on the schools of Western capitalist countries:

The more cultured was a bourgeois State, the more subtly it deceived, asserting that the school can remain outside of politics and thus serve society as a whole. In reality the school was wholly an instrument of class domination in the hands of the bourgeoisie; it was throughout permeated with the spirit of caste; and its aim was to give to the capitalists obliging serfs and competent workers.

In the communist State, the school is to be, quite frankly, an instrument of class domination in the hands of the proletariat, and there is to be no moral teaching other than what is useful to the workers in the class struggle. Lenin is quoted again as saying:

We deny any kind of morality which is taken from the non-human and non-class conception; and we regard such morality as a fraud and a deception which blocks the minds of workers and peasants in the interests of landowners and capitalists. We say that our morality is entirely subservient to the interests of the class struggle of the proletariat.

It would seem to follow that when the proletariat has achieved definitive victory, so that there is no longer any class struggle, there will be no such thing as morality. Pinkevitch, however, allows a somewhat more positive ethic to appear when he says:

The aim of nurture and general instruction in Soviet Russia is to aid in the all-round development of a healthy, strong, actively brave, independently thinking and acting man, acquainted with the many sides of contemporary culture, a creator and a warrior in the interests of the proletariat and consequently in the final analysis in the interests of the whole of humanity.

180

By merely omitting the incidental reference to the proletariat in this passage we obtain a very definite ethic involving nothing distinctively communistic. But in the period of transition propaganda must play a large part; during this period "the aim is, so to speak, the indoctrination of the youth in the proletarian philosophy."

Pinkevitch recognizes that "from the point of view of character formation infancy and childhood are indisputably the most important periods of life." He holds that it would be desirable if infants could be cared for in institutions, not only for their own sakes, but also in order "to realize completely the socialistic State in which woman, liberated from petty, dulling, and unproductive toil, takes her place side by side with man." Both in infancy and in childhood he thinks the school a better influence than the family.

Our chief criticism of the contemporary school is that it deals with children who spend three-fourths of their time outside and away from the influence of the school, with children who come to school with certain information, certain habits, and at least a disposition towards a certain outlook upon the world. Without the slightest doubt the children's home, which boys and girls enter in infancy or early childhood and where they remain until the approach of manhood and womanhood, provides a more perfect form of education. . . . In the children's home we can create without hampering circumstance the kind of educative environment to which we teachers of to-day aspire. But in ordinary day-schools, because of the superior strength of the home and other outside influences, we often find ourselves powerless.

The aspirations of the Soviet Government are made clear by these passages, but for the present they are no more than aspirations, and only 4 or 5 per cent. of children of pre-school age attend any kind of institution. Universal compulsory education, at present, is confined to the four years from eight to twelve, which are spent in the primary school.

⟨Throughout the period of education, whether long or short, the Russian school differs from that of other countries in being much less academic, much less narrowly concentrated on the imparting of knowledge. "Knowledge must not be the aim; it must rather be the natural and incidental product of a definite organization of the life of the children in the school.⟩In truth we must make our school a 'school of life.'" "In its work the school must be connected most intimately with reality; a prominent place must be given to productive labour; the entire structure of the school must promote the development of the social instincts and provide a socialistic training of the revolutionary communists of the future." Children in school do not only lessons, but useful manual work, so far as their strength and skill permit; and they do this not as education but as part of the duty of a citizen. Pinkevitch speaks of "the tremendous social and political rôle of labour in the school. . . . As long as labour is looked upon as something utilitarian or valuable from the point of view of motor training we shall not have a school which merits the name of socialistic or communistic.

182

Our pupil must feel himself a member of and a worker in a labouring society." This is one of the most important features in Russian education.

Pinkevitch does not tell, in as much detail as could be wished, exactly what labour children perform, and how many hours of the curriculum are occupied by it. "Regular occupations in actual production in factory or mill," he says, "are a part of the manual work of the school in the sense that they are closely articulated with the teaching program." In rural districts work on farms takes the place of work in factories. As to this, Julian Huxley says truly:[1]

This association of rural schools with farms has much more to be said for it than that of urban schools with factories. For agriculture is a broad subject, while each factory deals only with one specialized branch of industry; agriculture is more nearly coterminous with country life than industry with life in the city. And the dovetailing of the school with the farm as an integral part of a single institution is good from the educational point of view.

This point of view, however, is radically different from that of Soviet educators, who conceive the labour of school children rather in the light of a moral discipline. "While studying is necessary," says Pinkevitch, "the teaching of practical life activities is no less essential. In a socialistic labour school these activities must be social, and therefore useful. . . . Are we to regard socially useful work as work of a social character which is useful to the school and its

[1] *A Scientist Among the Soviets*, p. 102.

pupils, or as work of the school which is useful to the surrounding community? To our way of thinking the entire meaning of the problem depends on the acceptance of the second interpretation." That is to say, the labour of the children is to be ordinary necessary work, not special work selected on account of its educational value.

Socially useful work in the school is divided into two main departments, the first consisting of agitation and propaganda, the second of practical work. Under the former heading children are to agitate on a great variety of topics, e.g. for rotation of crops, for the "most worthy" candidates in elections, against religion, malaria, bed bugs, smoking and drunkenness. Practical work shows a similar diversity. Children are to engage in disinfecting grain with formaline, in combating ravines by tree-planting, in putting electric light into the homes of peasants, in distributing election literature, in reading newspapers to illiterates, in exterminating parasites, and in aiding needy widows.

The Soviet school aims not only at understanding the world but at transforming it; its purpose, as Pinkevitch states, is "the reconstruction of the world in accordance with the theory of Marx." The whole conception of passive cognition is foreign to the system; this must be remembered if the system is to be fairly judged.

I think it was as Russians rather than as Marxists that the Thirty-Fifth All Russian Conference on

Pre-School Education adopted the following resolution: "Music should penetrate completely the life of the child. There should be music during work, music during play, and music during holidays. The teacher should take into consideration the personal creativeness of the child and by organizing an orchestra and collective singing should provide him with the necessary musical experiences." This is admirable, but I cannot believe that a communist revolution would make the English equally musical.

The war mentality, which is necessary in Russia owing to the hostility of other countries to communism, has introduced into education a number of features which are closely similar to those which patriotism has produced elsewhere. The "Young Pioneers" are a copy of the Boy Scouts, and have closely similar laws and vows. Their laws are:

(1) The Pioneer is true to the cause of the working class and to the covenants of Lenin.
(2) The Pioneer is the younger brother and helper of the *Komsomol* and Communist.
(3) The Pioneer is a comrade to Pioneers and to the workers' and peasants' children of the world.
(4) The Pioneer organizes the surrounding children and participates with them in the environing life: the Pioneer is an example to all children.
(5) The Pioneer strives for knowledge. Knowledge and skill are power in the struggle for the workers' cause.

The Pioneers also take a solemn oath:

"I, a Young Pioneer of the Soviet Union, in the presence of my comrades solemnly promise that:

185

(1) I will firmly defend the cause of the working class in the struggle for the liberation of the workers and peasants of the world; (2) I will honourably and unfalteringly carry out the covenants of Lenin and the laws and customs of the Young Pioneers."

Although we are explicitly told that the Soviet Government does not believe in "moral" education, there is a distinct flavour of morality, one might say of priggery, about these laws and vows. The picture of the Young Pioneer striving for knowledge and being an example to all children recalls the pious children's books of my youth.

To those who have listened to reactionary propaganda it will come as a surprise to find that the Soviet attitude on sex education is far from radical. "The rôle of the teacher and parent," says Pinkevitch, "is to safeguard the child against undue stimulation of the sex interest." The energy of the young "should be directed towards physical culture, athletic sports, manual labour, intellectual activity, the Pioneer movement, and all forms of social work which require a considerable amount of physical power. If the strength of the child is expended normally in these directions, no strength for the hypertrophic development of the sex impulses will remain." Co-education is approved of as diminishing the sex attraction between boys and girls. Information on sexual subjects should not be excessive, since, if it is, "the result can only be the stimulation of an unhealthy and, one can suppose,

186

an insufficiently chaste attitude towards the sex relationship." He repudiates with horror a suggestion that children should observe coitus in dogs, chickens, cattle, and horses, and says: "If questions of sex are not singled out for separate and special emphasis, the attention of children and adolescents will not be fixed upon them." He holds that sex questions should be subordinated to "other more interesting and important problems." All this may be sound or unsound, but it shows nothing attributable to the Revolution. Except for the advocacy of co-education, which can hardly be called subversive, the views expressed are in substantial agreement with those of English Headmasters.

To estimate the prospects of education under communism from the present practice in Russia is not easy. Not only are there important respects in which the intentions of the Government have not yet been carried out, but, what is more important, the war mentality produced by the world-wide struggle between capitalism and communism so dominates the schools that it is difficult to foresee how they would develop if communism were everywhere victorious. I have not myself been in Russia since 1920, when little had been done. At that time I saw nursery schools where the children were happy and the physical care was excellent, but where they were exposed to intensive propaganda as soon as they could speak. I saw schools for older boys, which were doing their best in spite of an appalling

187

lack of equipment. I spoke with university professors, whose position was far from agreeable. But this experience is of little use in view of subsequent developments, as to which, however, I have had the advantage of first-hand reports.

In regard to religion and sex there seems to be, at present, little difference between Russian and Western schools. The religion taught is not the same, but it is taught with equal dogmatism. In Russia, as in the West, there are propositions which must be believed blindly, not subjected to critical scrutiny. It is true that the Russian religion, unlike that of Christian countries, is one which most young people who are exposed to it accept enthusiastically and make the basis of their lives. It is true that intelligent people can regard the Russian religion as a means towards the creation of a better world, and can accept its dogmas, at least pragmatically, without intellectual abdication. In these respects, Marxism has now the advantage which Christianity had when it was young, but would it retain these advantages if it were established and victorious? It is associated, for the moment, with the hopefulness and the fruitful activity due to the existence of a vast half-empty country ripe for economic development. America was at one time in that condition, and was then the protagonist of democracy. All progressive Europeans felt at that time an enthusiasm for America and for democracy, to which they attributed virtues which we can now see to have been connected with the existence of a continent awaiting exploitation. A similar geographical accident now operates in favour of communism, and we must discount its effect before we can estimate the results which communism would be likely to have in economically developed countries, where it could hardly give rise to the prolonged optimism which has characterized Russia in recent years.

If the Marxism dogma remains as virulent as it is at present, it must, in time, become a great obstacle to intellectual progress. Already there are aspects of modern science which communists find it difficult to reconcile with their theology, for example, the views as to the atom to which quantum theory has led. The opinion that everything in human character has economic causes may, at any moment, come into violent conflict with science. For example: hookworm greatly diminishes energy in warm countries, and in this matter climate, not economics, is the decisive factor. Moreover, the whole Marxian philosophy is so much concerned with the class struggle that it becomes vague and indefinite when it contemplates the class-less world that it aims at creating. If a conquering dogmatic Marxism were to replace Christianity, it might be as great an obstacle to scientific progress as Christianity has been.

It seems improbable, however, that the philosophy at present associated with communism would retain its force if communism were victorious. Com-

189

munism is, in itself, merely an economic system, which is to be judged on economic and political grounds. The doctrine of dialectical materialism and the economic interpretation of history are not logically necessary parts of communist theory. If communism as an economic system were no longer challenged, there would not be the same necessity for the suppression of heresy: Marx and Lenin, no doubt, would still be venerated, but it would be discovered that they had not meant what they said. Present-day dogmatism is an incident in the struggle, and we may hope that it would gradually fade away if the struggle were brought to a successful issue.

Similar considerations apply as regards the conflict of classes. The education in capitalist countries suffers, as we saw, from the domination of the rich, and the education in Russia suffers, conversely, from the domination of the proletariat. Children of proletarians are taught to despise children of "bourgeois," and young people of "bourgeois" origin have more difficulty than others in obtaining higher education. But within a generation this trouble will have disappeared, since there will no longer be any but proletarian children.

A more serious question, as regards the future, is the virtual abolition of the family. It is to be expected that, when funds permit, the Soviet Government will gradually cause more and more children to be educated wholly in institutions, and to have little or no contact with their parents. The advantages and disadvantages of this system have been considered in an earlier chapter, and I shall not repeat them, but for good or evil this is probably the most important feature in fully developed communist education.

There are several features in which education under communism is already preferable to any that is possible in capitalist countries. One of these is the mitigation of competition and the substitution of group activities for individual work. It is true that isolated progressive schools can attempt this in such countries as England and America, but they are handicapped by the necessity of preparing children for examinations and for the competitive struggles of adult life. Moreover, the children educated in exceptional schools are liable to have some difficulty in adapting themselves to the environment—a difficulty which may be worth enduring, but from which the Russian child is exempt. A school which aims at creating a peculiar environment must be more or less isolated from the ordinary world, which is regrettable even when it is necessary. In Russia competition is eliminated not only from the school but from daily life, which makes possible the creation of a co-operative spirit unknown in the West.

The participation of the school in the ordinary work of the world, though it has its dangers, has advantages which, to my mind, outweigh all possible drawbacks. At present, there is too much

191

propaganda in the work that children are expected to do: they are made, at an early age, into missionaries of the communist faith, which cannot fail to induce a certain smugness and undesirable self-assurance. But it is good for young people to feel themselves part of the community, and to have the sense that they ought to be useful so far as their capacities permit. Progressive educators in the West have, I think, been inclined to generate self-importance in the child, and to let him feel himself a little aristocrat whom adults must serve. This leads him to grow up an anarchist, impatient of the restraints of social life. From this defect, Russian education is free: the child is made to feel, from the first, that he is a unit in society and has a duty to the community. And he is made to feel this, not so much by precept, but rather by the ordering of his activities. This behaviouristic part of moral education in Russia is admirable, and has, if testimony is to be believed, the consequence that even the ablest of young men feel themselves part and parcel of the community, not, as they too often do in the West, isolated units who become frivolous through despair or predatory from cynicism. Communism has discovered a moral discipline which modern youth can accept, and a way of life in which modern youth can be happy. Capitalist countries are finding this problem insoluble, because their institutions cannot be preserved without humbug.

To the intellectual educated in the rich and

complex culture of an old civilization, there is, it must be confessed, something thin and almost intolerably monotonous in the communist outlook. The practice of referring all questions, however remote, to the class war vulgarizes everything, and destroys the pleasure in mental skill. Any illustration from pure science will serve to show what I mean; take, for example, the methods by which the distances of remote stars and nebulæ are estimated. These methods are a masterpiece of ingenuity, and of careful reasoning combined with accurate observation. So far as I know, it makes little difference to the issue of the class struggle whether the distance of a given star is a hundred or a thousand light-years, but it increases our respect for the human race that men should be able to decide which of these is nearer to the truth. I am not suggesting that communism would put a veto on astronomical research, but I am suggesting that its philosophy, if genuinely believed, would atrophy the impulse of scientific curiosity which leads men to such investigations. The Marxian outlook leads to a wrong emphasis. The work of Newton, for example, may have had all sorts of economic causes, but the work itself is far more interesting and important than its causes. Economics, after all, has to do with the problem of keeping alive; if this problem were satisfactorily solved, as it could be through communism, we should need something else to think about, and some new principle upon which to interpret *future* history. Simplicity is a merit in a slogan, but not in a philosophy.

Everything deliberately planned is likely to suffer from undue simplicity, leading to monotony, and even to a kind of insanity from perpetually hearing the same note struck. It may be that life itself will avoid this danger; at any rate, in Russia, there is still so much surviving from before the Revolution that communist planning cannot introduce undue simplicity for a long time to come. But in education, if there were not such obvious and interesting practical tasks to be accomplished, the danger of over-simplification would be very real. The world is more rich and varied than the Marxian formula. A generation confined within the philosophy of *Das Kapital* may be useful, happy, and formidable, but cannot be wise, and cannot know that it is not; intellectually, it will be cocksure and shallow. But in saying this I am speaking from the standpoint of philosophy, not of politics.

From the standpoint of politics (in the widest sense) I think our verdict must be different. Communism offers a solution of the difficult problem of the family and sex-equality—a solution which we may dislike, but which does, at any rate, provide a possible issue. It gives children an education from which the anti-social idea of competition has been almost entirely eliminated. It creates an economic system which appears to be the only practicable alternative to one of masters and slaves. It destroys

194

that separation of the school from life which the school owes to its monkish origin, and owing to which the intellectual, in the West, is becoming an increasingly useless member of society. It offers to young men and women a hope which is not chimerical and an activity in the usefulness of which they feel no doubt. And if it conquers the world, as it may do, it will solve most of the major evils of our time. On these grounds, in spite of reservations, it deserves support.

CHAPTER XIV

EDUCATION AND ECONOMICS

In public education as it exists at the present day
in Western countries we have found, in previous
chapters, various features which called for criticism.
There are those who hold that whatever is amiss
in education, or, for that matter, in anything else,
has its source in a bad economic system. I do not
myself believe this; I incline to the view that under
any economic system there will be a certain amount
of stupidity and a certain amount of love of power,
each of which will stand in the way of the creation
of a perfect educational system. Nevertheless, the
influence of economic factors on education is undoubtedly profound, and not always superficially
obvious. I shall endeavour, in this chapter, to
isolate the economic factor in education at various
times and in various countries.

European education, when it first revived after
the Dark Ages, was the prerogative of the priesthood, and to this day it has characteristics which
it owes to its ecclesiastical origin. Before the Renaissance, the lay aristocracy had, in general, little
knowledge, but the clergy, and especially the regular clergy, not infrequently possessed considerable
erudition. A certain slight knowledge of Latin was
a professional necessity, but this bare minimum

196

would not have amounted to much. It was mainly contact with the Moors, especially in Sicily and Spain, that caused the revival of learning in the eleventh, twelfth, and thirteenth centuries. And while this contact had, of course, causes which were largely economic, its effect upon learning must be attributed in the main to disinterested intellectual curiosity on the part of a rather small number of individuals.[1] Scholastic philosophy, and mediaeval learning generally, were due to the enthusiasm of a minority of ecclesiastics, most of whom derived little pecuniary advantage from their labours, while not a few incurred discredit by the boldness of their speculations. The existence of monks and friars was necessary for the movement, but its primary cause was the mere thirst for knowledge.

On the education of aristocratic laymen, which began somewhat later, the same may be said. The Emperor Frederick II, with whom secular culture may be taken to begin, had been in contact with the Mahometans from his earliest youth, and was devoured by an insatiable curiosity concerning everything ascertainable. The revival of Greek in Italy in the fifteenth century, and the courtly culture which spread thence to the northern nations, is to be attributed, in its inception, to love of learning for its own sake. It is true that this motive was soon submerged: knowledge of Latin and some

[1] See *The Legacy of Israel* (Oxford University Press), by various authors, pp. 204 ff.

197

knowledge of Greek became the mark of a gentleman, and was forced upon boys, with the result
that men lost the taste for it. Even then, however,
the motive for acquiring classical learning was snobbish rather than economic: no landowner ceased
to receive his rents if he failed to acquire culture.
The aristocrat, like the monk, was a man of leisure,
and could, if he chose, learn for pleasure, without
any utilitarian purpose.

Although the conception of knowledge as a thing
desirable on its own account still lingers in universities, and among a few belated philosophers (of
whom I am one), various things have happened
which have completely changed the current view
as to the function of education. The most important
of these is the establishment of universal compulsory instruction. It was found that boys and girls
could be turned into better citizens and more efficient workers if they knew how to read and write
than if they did not. It is true that, in pursuing
this aim, statesmen were hampered by the scholastic
tradition: the education in elementary schools is
almost purely bookish, although it might be argued
that a semi-practical training would have best
served the statesmen's purpose. In this respect,
Russian education is better adapted to the age.
Nevertheless, the elementary schools have, on the
whole, done what was wanted of them, and are
now, in every civilized country, one of the essential
instruments of government.

Another factor tending to a utilitarian view of education has been the growth of science and industry. Technical processes nowadays demand scientific knowledge, and new inventions are a source both of wealth and of national greatness. In this respect also, the traditions of an earlier age have prevented complete adaptation to present need except in Russia. If education were governed wholly by utilitarian considerations, the place of science and industrial technique would be much larger than it is, and the place of literary culture would be much smaller. But although this has not yet happened completely, it is happening by degrees, and will have happened completely before very long.

The influence of economic causes upon education may be dealt with under five heads, which we will consider successively.

First: According to the economic circumstances of a State, the amount of money which it can afford to spend on education will vary. But for the enrichment of the Western nations through the Industrial Revolution, universal compulsory education would have been impossible. No country has ever had a greater respect for learning than existed in China before the Chinese had adopted Western standards, but China was not rich enough to teach reading and writing to more than 5 per cent. of the population. In the England of 1780, or even of 1830, it would have been very difficult to impose

199

new taxation sufficient to provide schooling for everybody. At present, it is still considered impossible to provide nursery schools except in a few rare instances. The raising of the school-leaving age, on the other hand, is not thought to raise economic difficulties. Owing to unemployment and protectionism, practical men are agreed that everybody's work makes everybody else poorer, so that it is a benefit to the community to keep any section of it away from productive employment. On this ground it is thought that we should all be richer if children were kept longer at school. In England, the obstacle to raising the school age is not economic, but theological: the sects cannot agree as to the brand of superstition with which boys and girls shall be sent out into the world.

Second: One of the purposes of education is to increase total production. This was probably the principal motive in the minds of those who first introduced universal education, and it is undoubtedly a sound motive. A population that can read and write is more efficient than one that cannot. But the motive of maximizing production operates even more directly in promoting technical education, scientific instruction, and research. The British Government spends very much less money on research than it would spend if it were actuated by sound financial calculation, the reason being that most civil servants have had a classical education and are ignorant of everything that a modern man

200

should know. Consider, for example, medical research. The average citizen is an expense to the community at the beginning and end of his life, but profitable during his working years. Children who die have been a sheer economic loss, and a diminution of mortality during the early years is therefore a gain to the State. Or, again, consider such a matter as economic entomology, which is of decisive importance in many branches of agriculture: the minuteness of our public expenditure on this subject must be regarded as wilful extravagance. I am saying nothing of the more obvious and well-advertised branches of industrial research, such as synthetic dyes, high explosives, poison gases, etc., some useful, some quite the reverse. The usefulness of scientific knowledge is, as yet, not realized even by most of the people who are considered educated; when it is, we may expect greatly increased scientific endowments and a much larger place for science in the curriculum of secondary schools.

Third: The system of distribution has a profound effect upon education, much greater than that of the two factors we have hitherto considered. The system of distribution determines the division of the community into classes, and wherever there are classes, different classes will receive different kinds of education. In a capitalist society, wage-earners get least education, and those who aim at entering a learned profession get most, while an intermediate

amount is considered suitable for those who are
going to be "gentlemen" or business men. As a
general rule, a boy or girl belongs to the same
social class as his or her parents. But those who win
scholarships by exceptional ability can rise from
the wage-earning class into the professional class.
By this means, in England, the best brains born
into the wage-earning class are politically sterilized,
and cease, as a rule, to be on the side to which
their birth would have assigned them. In this fluidity
of classes a plutocratic society differs from an aristocratic one; that is one reason why revolutions are
less apt to occur under plutocracies than under
aristocracies.

The economic system which its opponents call
"capitalism" is a complex one, and for our purposes
it is important to subject it to some degree of
analysis. There are, I should say, three chief sources
of wealth in the modern world outside the U.S.S.R.
First, the ownership of land and natural monopolies;
second, inheritance in the patriarchal family; third,
business enterprise. These three are not inseparably
connected; Henry George wished to abolish the
first, while leaving the second and third untouched;
in the Catholic secular priesthood, the first exists
and the third might exist, but the second is eliminated; certain anti-Semites, if one may judge by
their diatribes, would preserve the first and second,
while destroying the third. I think land-owning and
inheritance, both of which are survivals of the aristo-

cratic regime, are much more open to socialist criticism than business enterprise; where this last is the sole source of success, as, for example, in the case of Henry Ford, it is questionable whether it does as much harm as good to the community as a whole. And certainly the conception of class, as generally understood, is impossible apart from inheritance. In education, more especially, the important thing is that the children of the well-to-do have an education which is different from that given to the children of wage-earners. In America, where plutocracy is less affected than in Europe by the lingering remnants of aristocracy, business enterprise is commonly represented as the main source of wealth. This has an effect upon the mentality of the young which is quite different from that which occurs in a society when land-owning and inheritance are the socially prominent sources of wealth. It emphasizes individual effort, and is to that extent good; but it emphasizes effort in the form of competition, and is in this respect anti-social. Under a more just economic system there would not be competition of the present sort, nor would there be classes such as are familiar to us. It is true that there might still be competition of a kind, and there might still be different classes in a sense. But the kind and the sense would be very different from those to which we are accus-tomed. In a communist society there would be positions of power, and there would be positions in which the work was unusually pleasant. The men occupying these positions would in some sense form a higher class than those occupying positions involving little power and unpleasant work. And there would presumably be competition to obtain the posts involving more power and more pleasant work. But in a world without inheritance and paternal power, each individual would compete entirely on his own merits, and not with the unfair advantage of better educational opportunities. If he obtained a better education than his neighbour, that would be because he had shown himself better qualified to receive it, not because his father happened to be rich. Whatever justification of classes might exist in such a society would therefore be founded in each individual case upon intrinsic merit. A great violinist, for example, will always be superior to one who is mediocre, and will be more honoured even if he is not more highly paid. This degree of inequality and competition is unavoidable. The inequality is rooted in the nature of things, and the competition is necessary in order that difficult work may be performed by the most competent men. That is why the problem of over-education, which we considered in an earlier chapter, is a difficult one. Educational competition will, however, be much less poignant than it is at present when all have economic equality, and all have economic security, not only for themselves but for their children. It is inequality and insecurity that make competition so bitter at the present time, and when these elements are removed, the sting will be taken out of it.

With regard to patriotism, though other motives enter in, there is a connection with private property, though this is not immediately obvious, and does not exist in the consciousness of most individuals. It is a round-about connection, caused by the more predatory forms of capitalism. Undeveloped countries have two uses from the standpoint of the investor: as markets, and as sources of raw materials. In both respects they are more profitable when they are under the control of the State to which the investor belongs. French capital finds a profitable field of investment in North Africa; British capital in India; and American capital in Central America. In this way the investor who thinks of investing his money outside his own country becomes interested in imperialism, economically if not territorially, and finds that by suitable patriotic propaganda a considerable part of the expense of his enterprise can be shifted on to the shoulders of the tax-payer. This is the source of most of the patriotism of powerful nations, although the citizens who shout for the flag are, in general, unaware of the sinister forces that have led them to do so. The nationalism of the weaker nations is a defence against that of the predatory nations. In so far as they are resisting exploitation instead of practising it, they are momentarily in a better moral position than that of the stronger nations. But the sentiments generated in a weak nation which is fighting for independence are such that, as soon as it succeeds, it acquires all the vices which it had previously decried in its oppressors. Poland, after nearly two hundred years of subjection, acquired freedom, but saw no reason for not passing on to the Ukrainians the burdens which had previously been endured by Poles. Nationalism is vicious as a principle, and is not to be admired, even in nations fighting for their freedom. This is not to say that nations ought not to resist oppression. It is to say that they should resist it from an international and not a merely national standpoint. The evils of nationalism, whether in a strong or weak nation, are connected with private property. They are concerned with exploitation or with the resistance to exploitation. It is therefore reasonable to suppose that, if private capitalism were abolished, the sinister part played at present by nationalism in education would be considerably diminished, though it might not wholly disappear.

The fourth head in our consideration of the effect of economic causes on education is endowments. Wherever freedom of testamentary disposition exists, a man may leave his property to any object which is not considered contrary to public policy. Until recently, bequests for the propagation of rationalism were void in England, on the ground that rationalism is contrary to the public policy of a Christian country; now this is no longer the case. But although endowments for progressive objects may not be illegal, it is inevitable that endowments should, in the main, be a conservative force. They embody the wishes of men who are dead, often of men who have been dead for centuries. The Churches, the older universities, and many schools, depend to a greater or less extent upon ancient bequests. In America, endowments are largely recent, but, where they are, they come from eminent plutocrats, who are necessarily conservative and usually uneducated. They thus have a considerable effect in retarding progressive movements in education. A university president whose professors are suspected of radicalism is less likely to secure donations from philanthropic captains of industry than one whose colleagues show an unbroken front in favour of the *status quo*.

Endowments have a considerable effect in making the religious side of education more conservative than it would otherwise be. The connection of religion with private property arises through the fact that men leave their money to religious bodies, and that this secures, for centuries after their death, the propagation of the particular brand of superstition in which they believed. In England and Scotland, it is true, this can be altered by legislation. At the time of the Reformation, property left by the pious of the Middle Ages was diverted from its original purpose to the teaching of Anglicanism. When the property of the Free Churches

207

in Scotland was judicially decided to belong by law to the Wee Frees, the law was altered so that the bequests of bigoted Predestinarians could be used to teach doctrines from which Predestination had been abolished. But in America the Constitution forbids such legislation. If you leave your money to an institution devoted to the doctrine that the inhabitants of Kentucky are the Lost Ten Tribes, the money cannot be diverted from that use. And in England, although diversion is possible, it is rare. The Anglican Church, and the Roman Catholic Church, are wealthy bodies, whose income is only available to those who profess suitable doctrines. There is thus an enormous economic motive for holding the same opinions as were held by remote ancestors. For every intellectual progress there is an economic penalty: when Colenso discovered that the hare does not chew the cud, he was docked of his salary.

If there were no such things as religious endowments, it cannot be doubted that things would change much more quickly than they do. Even as it is, they change in fact more quickly than in form. There are many things which Anglican clergymen have to profess to believe, although it is open to them to say it is a mere profession, and no one thinks the worse of them if they do say so. Some parts of the body of Christian dogma have life at one time, and some at another. At the present time, for example, it is the view of most Christians that

Christ's observations on the subject of divorce are to be interpreted literally, while His sayings on such matters as non-resistance, abstinence from oaths, and giving of one's property to the poor, are to be interpreted figuratively, as meaning the opposite of what they say. But the question which parts of Christ's teaching it is permissible for a Christian to accept is a complicated one, which I shall not pursue further.

The fifth head in our consideration of economic influences on education is tradition. I do not mean tradition in general, which is a much wider matter; I mean tradition derived from some economic cause which operated in the past but does not operate in the present. Sexual morals, which are usually very conservative, afford the best illustration of this factor. In former days, when the world was less populous and infant mortality was high, couples performed a public service in having many children. Until education and the prohibition of child labour had made children a source of expense, children were often a pecuniary advantage to their parents. The sentiment against birth control and abortion had, in those days, a sound economic justification which is now lacking, but the sentiment persists because it has become associated with religion.

The patriarchal family clearly had an economic origin, since women could not hunt successfully during pregnancy and lactation. Until recent times women had little opportunity of making an inde-

o   209

pendent living, and were therefore forced to be dependent upon husbands or male relatives. The patriarchal family, involving support of wives and descent in the male line, led naturally to insistence on virtue in wives, enforced by very severe ethical and religious sanctions, and usually, in early civilizations, by the death penalty for women guilty of adultery. While the legal penalty became lighter, and finally disappeared except in a few outlying regions such as New York State, the ethical and religious censures remained. This part of the conventional code, as we saw, is incompatible, in practice though not in theory, with the claim for the equality of women with men. Where women can earn their own living, their claim to equality is irresistible. Frantic efforts are made to prevent married women from obtaining employment, but it is not to be supposed that these efforts can have much permanent success. There will also be an increasing number of ways in which a woman can make a living without being of impeccable virtue from a conventional standpoint. The existing moral code, therefore, is in process of breaking down from economic causes. Falling birth-rates, combined with militarism, are giving to the State an increasing interest in the welfare of children, since it is wasteful, from the governmental point of view, for a male to die before he is old enough to be killed on the battle-field. Where economic causes combine to diminish the virtue of women, and to increase the share of the State in the maintenance of children, it is clear that the importance of fathers must diminish, and with it all those sentiments and moral precepts that are bound up with the patriarchal family. At present, parents and the State combine in thinking it good for children to be taught an outlook on sexual matters which comes from the past, and is not well adapted to the world of the present. This is an example of the conservatism of sentiment where sex and family are concerned. This conservatism is especially strong as regards education, since most people are of opinion that it can do the young no harm to be taught a very strict morality. Education, therefore, tends to prevent societies from adapting themselves to new needs as quickly as they ought, and causes many adult men and women to feel a horror, derived from their early training, in regard to things which it would be well to accept as a matter of course. While, therefore, economic causes have played a part in producing the sex morality which is taught in schools, these causes lie in the past, and find no justification in the economic needs of the present day.

Although, as we have seen, economic causes connected with private property tend to make education conservative, it may be doubted whether it will be any less conservative under communism when once the revolutionary period is past. It will then be subject to completely unified bureaucratic control, and bureaucrats are not, as a rule, very eager for change. Perhaps there will then be less need of rapid change than there is now; perhaps mankind may be the better for a period of peaceful consolidation. However that may be, the substitution of co-operation for competition as an educational ideal will remain a solid moral advance, which only a complete change in the economic system renders possible. On this ground alone it is legitimate to hope that education under communism will produce better men and women than those that the West can produce while the present system persists.

CHAPTER XV

PROPAGANDA IN EDUCATION

(PROPAGANDA may be defined as any attempt, by means of persuasion, to enlist human beings in the service of one party to any dispute. It is thus distinguished from persecution by its method, which is one that eschews force, and from instruction by its motive, which is not the dissemination of knowledge but the generating of some kind of party feeling. It may differ from instruction in nothing but motive, since it may (though this is exceptional) consist entirely of accurate information; but even then it will consist of such information as tends in a given direction, to the exclusion of such as has a contrary tendency. Eulogy and invective, as opposed to scientific psychological analysis, are both propaganda, though most men have enough virtues and enough defects to enable either to dispense with falsehood. In like manner it is possible to write the history of a nation from a friendly or a hostile point of view, and to confine oneself, in doing so, to true statements: the impression conveyed to the reader is incorrect, but only through its omissions.

(In all education, propaganda has a part; no adult can avoid expressing his aversions and preferences, and any such expression in the presence of the young has the effect of propaganda. The question for the

213

educator is not whether there shall be propaganda, but how much, how organized, and of what sort; also whether, at some stage during education, an attempt should be made to free boys and girls, as far as possible, from the influence of propaganda by teaching them methods of arriving at impartial judgements.

The part played by propaganda in education has been continually increasing ever since the Reformation. The first to perfect its technique were the Jesuits, who, by acquiring control over education, consolidated the gains made in the counter-Reformation. But the Protestants were not far behind; in England, for example, the Spanish Inquisition, the fires of Smithfield, and the Gunpowder Plot, were utilized to the full. The eighteenth century, as contrasted with the seventeenth, was peaceful and fairly free from propaganda until the outbreak of the French Revolution. The wars of the eighteenth century, important as they were in their issue, were not very fierce, and did not prevent the combatants from respecting each other. But Jacobinism led to a sterner spirit in Europe, while in the long fight against Napoleon the English became insular and the Germans became patriotic. From that time to the present day the conflict between progress and reaction has grown more and more bitter, while nationalism has played an increasing part in the lives of ordinary men and women. At the present time different nations, and even different political

214

groups within the same nation, are completely separated, not only by their beliefs, but by what they know and do not know, by their judgements of prominent men, and by their hopes and fears for the future.

(Propaganda is first an effect, and then a cause, of the divisions which exist in the modern world. Before the Reformation there was a certain degree of unity in Europe; such heretics as existed were dealt with by persecution, and there was no necessity for propaganda in the modern sense. During the Wars of Religion, on the contrary, victory or defeat might turn on the power of making converts. The victory of France in the revolutionary wars was largely due to the energy and enthusiasm generated by Jacobin propaganda. Socialism and communism have been built up entirely by propaganda, and but for patriotic propaganda the nations would not have endured the sacrifices demanded of them in the Great War.

(Universal education has increased immeasurably the opportunities of propaganda. Not only is education itself everywhere propagandist, but the power of reading makes the whole population susceptible to the influence of the Press. This was the principal reason why the late war was more bitter than previous wars. People who had learnt to read, but had learnt nothing else, could be influenced by stories of atrocities, whereas in former times most people had either no education or a good deal, and

215

were in either case comparatively immune. As this instance shows, propaganda has now an importance that it never had before.

⟮The main forms of propaganda are three: for political parties, for creeds, and for nations. The first of these cannot be overtly undertaken by the State, which can, however, engage in propaganda against very small parties, such as the communists in England and America. Propaganda for political parties is, in the main, not conducted in the course of education. Of course the atmosphere of a school for the rich is conservative, but most of the children would in any case grow up conservative, so that there is not much need of party propaganda. Creeds and nations are considered proper matters for propaganda in schools. Roman Catholics prefer to have their children educated in Roman Catholic schools; Protestants prefer a mild religious atmosphere which approximately expresses their beliefs. Every great nation causes a spirit of nationalism to permeate the State schools, and considers this one of the most valuable parts of the education of ordinary citizens. Under communism, nationalism is not taught, but there is a very intense propaganda for communism, combined with the information that the U.S.S.R. is its protagonist. It may be doubted whether the effect upon the minds of the children differs very greatly from the nationalism produced by education in capitalist countries.

⟮Propaganda in education is usually successful in

its object, unless there is some special reason for failure. The great majority of mankind accept the religion in which they were brought up, and the patriotism that they learnt at school. Children of immigrants in the United States become patriotic Americans, and usually despise their parents' country of origin; this is mainly the effect of the schools. The only thing that causes nationalist propaganda to fail on a large scale is defeat in war. Most Russians ceased to be patriotic in 1917, and many Germans ceased in 1918; most of these last, however, were compelled by the Treaty of Versailles to abandon internationalism. Propaganda will not fail, as a rule, unless it attempts to make people believe something against which they have a strong initial repugnance. It was not found possible to make the Southern Irish feel British patriotism or adopt the Protestant religion. If propaganda is to succeed, it must inculcate something which makes some kind of instinctive appeal; in that case, it can enormously increase the virulence of group feeling. Where some hatred already exists, it can intensify it; where some superstitious feeling lurks, it can seize hold of it and make it dominant; where a love of power is dormant, it can awaken it. But there are limits to what can be done by propaganda, both for good and evil. At least as yet that is the case; perhaps, when mass psychology has been perfected, there will be no limits to what governments can make their subjects believe.)

Propaganda may be concerned with values, or with general propositions, or with matters of fact. Somewhat different considerations apply to these three cases.

Ultimate values are not matters as to which argument is possible. If a man maintains that misery is desirable, and that it would be a good thing if everybody always had violent toothache, we may disagree with him, and we may laugh at him when we catch him going to the dentist, but we cannot prove that he is mistaken, as we could if he said that iron is lighter than water. If a prophet were to advance the theory that happiness should be confined to those whose first name begins with Z, he might receive the enthusiastic support of an army of Zacharys and Zedekiahs and Zebedees, but would ultimately be defeated by the solid legions of Johns and Georges. This would, however, be only a pragmatic refutation of the prophet's message, which would remain logically just as good as its contradictory. (As to ultimate values, men may agree or disagree, they may fight with guns or with ballot-papers, but they cannot reason logically.)

In practical life, questions as to ultimate values hardly ever arise in their logical purity, since men are concerned with what should be *done*. (Whether an act should be performed depends upon two considerations: first, what its effects are likely to be; second, whether these effects are on the whole good, or, more accurately, whether, on the balance, they are better than the effects of any other act which is possible in the circumstances. Of these two questions, the first is scientific, not ethical, and is amenable to rational argument, like every other scientific question. It is only when a dispute as to what should be done turns on the second question that there is no theoretical possibility of deciding it by argument.

In political disputes there tend to be two disagreements, one nominal, the other real. Every man, left to the unaided operation of instinct, would hold that his own happiness is the supreme good, that of his family comes next, while that of his nation, his party, and his co-religionists is to be desired so long as it does not conflict with his own. If he is an absolute monarch, he may retain this opinion through life. But if he is not (which is, after all, the commoner case), he can only get his way by the help of allies, and he can only acquire allies by at least appearing to pursue some object common to him and them. As a rule, this appearance will be partly genuine, partly not. In so far as it is not genuine, it depends in part upon the generating of emotion, in part upon fallacious reasoning. The part played by fallacious reasoning is larger than many modern irrationalists suppose. For example: from the end of the war until the autumn of 1931, British industry was sacrificed to British banking, because the bulk of British industrialists were persuaded by fallacious arguments advanced

219

by British bankers. Every political party, while it genuinely represents the interests of some group, endeavours to prove, by means of argument, that it represents the interests of other groups also; or, if no plausible argument is possible, it endeavours to produce the same result by means of excited emotion. In either case, disputes as to ultimate values do not occur, since no political party dare baldly avow the egoism of the group whose interests it is formed to further. Every political party asserts that it aims at the greatest possible happiness for the whole community, if not in this world, then in the next. Questions of ultimate ethical values, therefore, may be ignored in their intellectual form, though in emotional forms they retain political importance.

From what has been said it follows that there is a considerable region, in political disputes, which is open to scientific argument. When one group contends that its interests are really identical with those of another, its contention can always in theory, and sometimes in practice, be proved or disproved. Imperialist nations maintain that backward nations (i.e. those without powerful armed forces) are happier under their domination than they would be if they were free. Until women had the vote, men maintained that women were happier under male government than in a regime of sex equality. Captains of industry maintain that wage-earners, under their wise direction, are more prosperous than they would be if industry were subjected to public management. Such arguments generally convince a certain percentage of the subject group to which they are addressed; but as, in this case, they are not backed by self-interest, it is possible, when they are fallacious, to make this fact evident by argument. And even the dominant group will lose self-assurance if its conviction of its own rightness can be shaken. Many French aristocrats in 1789, many Russian aristocrats in 1917, doubted whether the privileges of their order were justified, and but for this doubt the French and Russian Revolutions would have had more difficulty in succeeding.

So much for the intellectual aspects of questions of value. In practice, however, the methods employed in ethical propaganda are emotional rather than intellectual. Seeing that all judgements of value are based, in the last analysis, upon emotions, it is natural that ethical propaganda should be emotional. Nevertheless there are distinctions to be made as to the kinds of emotion that are generated and as to the methods by which this is done.

Emotional propaganda may be direct or indirect. *Uncle Tom's Cabin* is direct propaganda; so is *Ye Mariners of England*. In direct propaganda, the object concerned is described in such terms as to rouse towards it the emotions desired by the propagandist. Indirect propaganda consists in arousing emotions, in themselves unconnected with the object, in circumstances which establish an association with the object. This is the function of Church music, and of all music which is used in connection with some social group. The love that upper-class Englishmen feel for their public school is a complex sentiment, largely due to the fact that various strong social emotions have been felt in school crowds; this sentiment is sufficiently powerful to last through life and to have considerable political importance. The sentiment of Roman Catholics for the Church is bound up with the emotions that they felt in youth at midnight mass, at the solemnity of Good Friday and the joyfulness of Easter, at incense and darkness and mystery. When strong childish or adolescent emotions of this sort become associated with a political group, they may, and often do, generate a sentiment which is capable of overriding all intellectual convictions. This form of propaganda is best understood by the Catholic Church, which has had nearly two thousand years in which to perfect its technique. But the same sort of thing is done, though less perfectly, by national States, in such forms as martial music and military displays. In my childhood, British soldiers still wore the traditional red coats, and I remember vividly the delight of seeing regiments on the march. Such delights tend, unless counteracted, to produce a belief in militarism.

Emotional propaganda has several dangers.(In the first place, it is just as easily used in a bad cause as in a good one, perhaps more easily. Indeed, since rational conduct generally involves some con-

222

trol of the emotions, a form of propaganda which consists in arousing rather simple and uncivilized emotions cannot but be an obstacle to sensible behaviour. When war is coming, men rejoice that they can let their barbaric emotions have free play; they experience a delight not wholly unlike that which a usually sedate person experiences when he falls in love. Both religion and patriotism appeal to very primitive emotions, which are dangerous to civilization. If men are to live closely packed together, they must have a careful social organization, and restrain their instinctive hostility to one another. The maintenance of so large a population as civilized countries at present contain is impossible if free rein is given to uncivilized passions, and therefore civilized men have a certain discomfort, an itch to return to more primitive ways of feeling, to which the emotional propagandist appeals. War and religion are the politically most important forms of this kind of nostalgia.

(Another danger of emotional propaganda is that it tends to close the mind to argument. The conscious mind may be rational, but just below the level of consciousness unalterable convictions remain from early years. Many men, in quiet times, are internationalists and freethinkers, but when there is danger of war or death they become patriotic or religious. This, of course, is only partly due to early propaganda; in a great measure, it is a natural effect of fear. But propaganda plays its part in enabling

223

fear to disguise itself as something more respectable, such as love of country or love of God.

Propaganda in regard to general propositions, such as religious dogmas, is conducted mainly by emotional means. To the Catholic, for example, emotions which he cherishes are associated with the Catholic faith, so that without belief in certain metaphysical statements he would be unhappy. Where belief in a creed is concerned, it is, of course, theoretically possible to combat it by purely intellectual means, but this will not be successful except with a small percentage of exceptionally rational people. In general, when large numbers of men and women have abandoned a creed in which they had grown up, there has been some economic motive at work, though often unconsciously. The Reformation would not have had the success it had but for the Church lands and the tribute exacted by Rome. Socialists on the Continent have been, in the main, anti-Christian and have offered economic arguments to show that Christianity is in the interests of the rich. It is seldom that any religious creed has been successfully combated by logic; perhaps French eighteenth-century rationalism is the most important instance. It is, however, desirable that reason should play a larger part than it does in determining men's convictions, or absence of convictions, on such matters as dogmatic religion deals with. The propaganda that attaches emotions, especially praise or blame to belief or disbelief in certain propositions, is an obstacle to the scientific spirit, and therefore to civilization.

Although it is scarcely probable that governments will adopt the expedient of exposing the young to propaganda from opposite sides on important vexed questions, I have no doubt that this would be the best plan if it could be introduced. To demand of a teacher that he shall abstain altogether from expressing controversial opinions is to demand that he shall be dull and shall suppress half his personality. There are those, it is true, who have no party feelings, but they seldom make inspiring teachers. Nor is it desirable that education should artificially avoid all the questions upon which contemporary events turn. Young people should be encouraged to think about such questions by hearing them discussed from every point of view. Communism should be debated on the wireless on alternate Mondays by the Soviet Ambassador and Mr. Winston Churchill; school-children should be compelled to listen, and after the debate had lasted three months each school should take a free vote. On Tuesdays, India should be debated between Gandhi and the Viceroy; on Wednesdays, Christianity, between Stalin and the Archbishop of Canterbury. This would be a real preparation for taking part in a democracy, and would teach the difficult art of extracting the truth from an *ex parte* statement. It is not propaganda as such that is at fault, but one-sided propaganda.

To be critical of propaganda, to have what is called in America "sales resistance," is highly desirable, and is not to be achieved by remoteness from propaganda, any more than immunity from measles is achieved by remoteness from measles. It is achieved by experiencing propaganda and discovering that it is often misleading. For this purpose, no plan could be so suitable as rival propagandists in every school, for which broadcasting supplies the mechanism.

(It must, I think, be admitted that a certain amount of uncompensated propaganda is necessary for the minimum of social cohesion. While there may be occasions when law-breaking is a duty, they are few, and on the whole respect for law is desirable. If wars are ever to be avoided, there will have to be international machinery to settle disputes, and it will be necessary to teach respect for the body that makes the settlements. It might be argued by a pacifist that it is not the existence of propaganda that does the harm, but the existence of opposite kinds of propaganda; if, instead of each nation teaching its own nationalism, all taught admiration for the United States, there would no longer be any occasion for conflict between nations; and if all economic teaching throughout the world were communistic, or if all were capitalistic, the conflict between the Soviet Government and the governments of the West would soon be terminated. So, I say, a pacifist might argue. But there would be several objections to such a plan. No progress would be possible in a world where only one doctrine on a doubtful subject could be taught. And there would be no training in critical judgement in a world where no topic was ever debated. Propaganda must therefore be as diversified as possible, both for the sake of progress and for the sake of education in weighing pros and cons; this is part of the objection to every kind of political censorship.

{One of the most important parts of education, and one of the most neglected, is that which teaches how to reach true conclusions on insufficient data. As a logician I am conscious of uttering what is, in strict logic, mere nonsense when I say this; nevertheless all success in practical life depends upon ability to perform this apparently impossible feat. The successful general is the one who guesses correctly what his opponent will do; the successful organizer is the one who can choose good subordinates after brief interviews. Even the successful man of science makes a guess which afterwards is verified. In politics, the data are hardly ever sufficient to enable a rational man to reach a reasoned conclusion, but they are often such as to enable a man who is both rational and shrewd to reach a sagacious conclusion. To do this requires the scientific absence of bias and power of hypothetical thought, but it requires also something else—that quality which is vaguely called "judgement." This is a quality which is greatly improved in any given direction by experience of the appropriate material.

227

Young people ought, at some stage in their education, to be taught political judgement, by listening to eloquence known in advance to be misleading, by reading partisan statements about past events and trying to infer what really happened, and so on. All this is the opposite of propaganda; it is the technique for rendering men immune to propaganda.

I am aware that, in what I have been saying, I have tacitly taken sides in a controversy which is very relevant to this issue. I have assumed that opinions can be true or false, not merely useful or harmful; I have assumed that it is, as a rule, at any rate where matters of fact are concerned, easier to know whether an opinion is true than whether it is useful; and, finally, I have assumed that, as a general rule, it is more useful to believe what is true than what is false. All these assumptions may be challenged, and are challenged by pragmatists and communists. Let us therefore examine them more closely.

(It is said that Caesar was killed on the Ides of March. I have not examined the evidence with any care, but I have read the statement in various books which appear reliable, and I therefore believe it. In youth it may be useful to believe it, since it may be a help in getting through examinations; but when once the period of examinations is passed, this belief ceases to serve any useful purpose. At any rate, to come to our second assumption, it is clearly easier to know the truth of the proposition "Caesar was killed on the Ides of March" than it is to know its utility, which, except to examinees, is extremely questionable. In saying this, I may seem to contradict my third assumption, namely, that as a general rule it is more useful to believe what is true than what is false. This is only correct when there is utility in one or other. Most propositions are not worth either believing or disbelieving. Imagine the multiplication table extended indefinitely to larger and larger numbers: it would contain an infinite number of propositions, of which only a finite number would be useful in practice. But whenever, for some reason, one of these propositions is needed, it is in the highest degree improbable that it will be better to get it wrong than right. It is not impossible, since you may have made a previous mistake which is just balanced by your new mistake. But this possibility is too remote to concern the politician, who rightly demands that children shall do their sums right.

The case of arithmetic would perhaps be conceded by the communist, but in regard to controversial opinions he would maintain that there is a bourgeois view and a proletarian view, and that every good soldier in the proletarian army must hold the proletarian view. Take, for example, the question of immortality. The way to deal with this question, a communist would say, is not to examine the relation of soul and body or the evidence accumulated by psychical research, nor yet to suspend judgement on the ground that the evidence is insufficient for a decision, but to observe that the promise of heaven hereafter is used to make proletarians content with their lot here below and satisfied with lower wages than they would otherwise demand. (The doctrine of immortality is thus made to appear as one of the weapons of capitalism, while its denial is one of the weapons of communism. The question of truth or falsehood does not enter in; one might as well ask whether a bullet is true or false. The important thing about a bullet is: which army does it serve? And exactly the same thing is what is important about an opinion.)

(This view is, of course, a negation of the scientific attitude, which is that, over a large region, it is possible to discover approximate truth, and that where this is not possible suspense of judgement is the only rational attitude. Moreover, the communist does not hold consistently to his own sceptical position. Dialectical materialism is held to be really true, not only what it is expedient for a proletarian to believe. And the proposition that such-and-such a belief is expedient for the proletarian is also held to be genuinely true; if it were not, it could not be made the basis of propagandist practice. The pragmatism of the communist is thus half-hearted, and little more than an expression of impatience.

I conclude that there are truths, that they can sometimes be known approximately, that this is often useful, and that belief in falsehood is very

230

rarely useful. I conclude, further, that it should be one of the purposes of education to teach the young to reach correct conclusions wherever possible. Failure to do this promotes the bitterness of party spirit and the danger of destructive conflict, while on the intellectual side it gravely impedes scientific progress. All these things statesmen would do well to remember when they are tempted to view education as a mere branch of political propaganda.

CHAPTER XVI

THE RECONCILIATION OF INDIVIDUALITY
AND CITIZENSHIP

In our first chapter we proposed a question: Can the fullest individual development be combined with the necessary minimum of social coherence? This has led us to consider the various ways in which education is affected by politics and economics, most of which, we have found, are harmful to the boys and girls concerned. Is it necessary that the effects of politics and economics on the individual should always be harmful? Or is this a temporary misfortune of our own time? And, in the latter case, what hope is there of a greater harmony between individuality and citizenship in the not too distant future?

⟮The harm that is done to education by politics arises chiefly from two sources: first, that the interests of some partial group are placed before the interests of mankind; second, that there is too great a love of uniformity both in the herd and in the bureaucrat. Of these two evils, the first is at present the greater; but if the first were overcome, the second might become very grave.

It has been the custom for education to favour one's own State, one's own religion, the male sex, and the rich. In countries where various religions exist side by side, the State is not able to favour any one of them in its schools, but this has led to the creation of schools belonging to various sects, or, as in New York City and Boston, to distortion, in the Catholic interest, of the history taught in the public schools.[1] The male sex can no longer be favoured as it used to be. But education, outside Russia, is still so conducted as to further the interests of the rich; and of course everywhere it teaches an exclusive loyalty to one's own State.

(The result of this state of affairs is that education has become part of the struggle for power between religions, classes, and nations. The pupil is not considered for his own sake, but as a recruit: the educational machine is not concerned with his welfare, but with ulterior political purposes. There is no reason to suppose that the State will ever place the interests of the child before its own interests; we have, therefore, to inquire whether there is any possibility of a State whose interests, where education is concerned, will be approximately identical with those of the child.

It is obvious that the first requisite for this purpose is the elimination of large-scale wars. If this were achieved by the establishment of an international authority, the teaching of militant nationalism would no longer serve any purpose, and would soon diminish to a point where it would be

[1] In New York City, for example, teachers have to speak of the Reformation as "the Protestant Revolt."

innocuous. There would no longer be any need for Officers' Training Corps, or for compulsory military service, or for the teaching of false history. Moral training would no longer have homicide as the apex of a virtuous life, to which everything else leads up. The establishment of an international authority sufficiently strong to impose its settlement of disputes upon recalcitrant States is, I am convinced, the most important reform from an educational as well as from every other point of view.

There are, however, formidable obstacles to the establishment of such an authority—obstacles much more formidable than most pacifists realize. Consider such an issue as that between communism and capitalism. It is extremely improbable that this issue will be settled peaceably: on both sides men consider it sufficiently vital to be worth fighting about, and it is difficult to imagine any international machinery strong enough to prevent it from leading to war. Imagine (say) a civil war in Germany between communists and nationalists. Would France and Russia look on passively? If France and Russia joined in, would Great Britain remain neutral? Would the United States risk the spread of communism over the whole Continent of Europe? Would China and India fail to profit by the opportunity? Until the issue between communism and capitalism is decided in one way or another, world peace cannot be secure, whatever machinery may be created. And it is difficult to see how this issue can be decided except by the victory of communism, at any rate throughout Europe. Capitalism will no longer bring contentment. Before very long, the general standard of comfort may be higher in Russia than elsewhere; the propagandist effect of such a state of affairs will be irresistible. It seems, therefore, not improbable that the shortest road to world peace lies through Russian propaganda. If so, it is short-sighted to object to the somewhat crude methods employed by the Soviet Government in teaching communism to its boys and girls. I do not positively assert all this; I merely suggest it as an hypothesis which is by no means improbable.

It is, of course, clear that there cannot be secure peace until Germany ceases to be punished for having been defeated in the war. And this will not happen until France ceases to dominate Europe. And France will perhaps not cease to dominate except as the result of a war.

It is doubtful, also, whether the liberation of India from the domination of England and of China from that of Japan can be achieved except through a first-class war.

All these large questions will have to be solved before there is any serious hope of the preservation of peace by the creation of an international authority. They may all be solved by the victory of communism within the next twenty years, but I am scarcely enough of an optimist to expect this.

(Next to the elimination of war, the most important requisite in the reconciliation of the individual
and the citizen is the elimination of superstition.
For this purpose, I define a belief as superstitious
if its sole basis is traditional or emotional. When
people consider the preservation of such beliefs
important, they create systems of education involving respect for the wisdom of our ancestors and a
habit of deciding questions on other than rational
grounds. Holders of power, almost inevitably, desire
their subjects to be emotional rather than rational,
since this renders it easier to make those who are
victims of an unjust social system contented with
their lot. Superstition thus becomes the natural ally
of injustice, and only where the economic and
political institutions are just is governmental education likely to promote a rational outlook.)

It is, of course, by no means certain that, if a
just economic system were established as the result
of a long conflict, it would, at first, be unaccompanied by superstition. In war-time, false beliefs are
used to generate enthusiasm, and a strict intellectual
discipline is found useful in preventing doubts as to
the importance of the cause. Russian communism
already has its body of theological dogma, its hagio-
logy, and its sacred history. If, after a century of
struggle, the Russian doctrine converts the world,
it will, in the interval, have created many myths
and acquired great doctrinal rigidity. The man who,
when that time comes, shall venture to say that

Marx and Lenin were not the greatest men that ever lived, is likely to be considerably persecuted. It is possible—though I do not think it is probable—that the communist party may come to occupy a position somewhat similar to that of the Church in the Dark Ages. It is possible that the wars preceding the victory of communism will destroy all the industrial plant in the world and cause the death of all men of science and competent technicians. In that case, when it is found recorded in the Scriptures that Lenin expected salvation from "Electrification," people may wonder what this word meant, and may conclude that it denoted mystic union with Karl Marx. It is, therefore, not inconceivable that there may come to be a world State with a just economic system and nevertheless dominated by superstition. But this can hardly happen except on the hypothesis of appallingly destructive wars. On any other hypothesis, it is to be expected that the elements of superstition which are at present associated with the Soviet Government will fade when victory has removed the need of a war mentality. In the long run, even a belief in communism will cease to seem important, since no other system will come within the purview of practical politics.

(I come now to a second danger, which is that of a too great love of uniformity. This may exist, as we said before, both in the bureaucrat and in the herd. Children are instinctively hostile to anything "odd" in other children, especially in the ages from ten to fifteen. If the authorities realize that this conventionality is undesirable, they can guard against it in various ways, and they can, as was suggested in an earlier chapter, place the cleverer children in separate schools. The intolerance of eccentricity that I am speaking of is strongest in the stupidest children, who tend to regard the peculiar tastes of clever children as affording just grounds for persecution. When the authorities also are stupid (which may occur), they will tend to side with the stupid children, and acquiesce, at least tacitly, in rough treatment for those who show intelligence. In that case, a society will be produced in which all the important positions will be won by those whose stupidity enables them to please the herd. Such a society will have corrupt politicians, ignorant school-masters, policemen who cannot catch criminals, and judges who condemn innocent men. Such a society, even if it inhabits a country full of natural wealth, will in the end grow poor from inability to choose able men for important posts. Such a society, though it may prate of Liberty and even erect statues in her honour, will be a persecuting society, which will punish the very men whose ideas might save it from disaster. All this will spring from the too intense pressure of the herd, first at school and then in the world at large. Where such excessive pressure exists, those who direct education are not, as a rule, aware that it is an evil; indeed, they are quite apt to welcome it as a force making for good behaviour. It is important, therefore, to consider what circumstances cause school-masters and education officials to fall into this error, and whether any system is likely to prevent them from doing so.

There are, in the teaching profession, two very different types. There are those who have an enthusiasm for some subject, and who love to teach it and implant their own enthusiasm in their pupils. On the other hand, there are those who enjoy the position of power and easy superiority, who like governing but have not enough skill to govern grown men. Some systems favour the former type, some the latter; modern efficiency tends more and more to favour the man who governs rather than teaches. I do not deny that the governing type has its uses: I once knew a lady who had taught in a public school in Texas, and had found it necessary always to come armed with a revolver. But except in remote and sparsely populated regions, boys or girls who are abnormally refractory can be isolated, with the result that those who remain, having lost their ringleader, will become amenable to less drastic methods. The teacher who is inspired by love of his subject, combined with affection for children, can in most circumstances achieve far more in the way of imparting knowledge and civilization than can ever be achieved by the man who loves order and method and efficiency but lacks knowledge and hates children. Unfortunately, in

239

any large school there is a considerable amount of
administrative routine, which is generally done best
by the worst teachers; and as the higher authorities see the administrative work but are apt not
to see the teaching, there is a tendency for credit
to be quite wrongly apportioned. Moreover, in any
great administrative machine the officials at the
head of it naturally consider administration the
most honourable and difficult kind of work, with
the result that a better status and a higher salary
are given to those who do the administrative work
of schools than to those who actually teach. All this
tends to produce the wrong type of teacher. It is
the executive type that encourages uniformity, while
the other type will rejoice in ability (which is in
itself an eccentricity), and for the sake of ability will
readily tolerate other forms of oddity.(It is therefore
very important, in combating the danger of uniformity, to encourage teachers who love teaching
rather than those who love governing.)

We come here upon one aspect of a problem
which is likely to grow increasingly serious as the
world becomes more organized.(A man who has
a position of power in a great organization requires
a definite type of ability, namely, that which is
called executive or administrative; it makes very
little difference what the matter is that the organization handles, the kind of skill required at the top
will be always the same. A man who can organize
successfully (let us say) the Lancashire cotton trade

240

will also be successful if he tackles the air defences of London, the exploration of Central Asia, or the transport of timber from British Columbia to England. For these various undertakings he will require no knowledge of cotton, no knowledge of aerial warfare, no knowledge of the buried cities of Turkestan, and no acquaintance with forestry or navigation. His helpers in subordinate positions will, in the several cases, require these several kinds of skill; but his skill is, in a sense, abstract, and does not depend upon specialized knowledge. It thus happens, as organizations increase in size, that the important positions of power tend, more and more, to be in the hands of men who have no intimate familiarity with the purposes of the work that they organize. While this is unavoidable, it has its dangers; and, to return to our theme, it has its dangers in the sphere of education.

In the sphere of education, the danger of the administrator arises through his love of classification and statistics. It is impossible that he should not have this passion, since he must deal quickly with vast masses of material, which only classification will enable him to do. Now in some kinds of material, classification is fairly satisfactory; this occurs where there are well-marked natural kinds. The greengrocer sells peas and beans and spinach and cabbage, and is never obliged to stop and ask himself: "Is this object a pea or a cauliflower?" With children the matter is otherwise. The question

Q   241

whether a given child is mentally deficient is often a border-line question, to which, speaking scientifically, no precise answer can be given. But speaking administratively, a precise answer *must* be given: the child must either be sent to a special school or kept in the ordinary school. The administrator, therefore, looks about for some means of reaching a precision which does not exist in nature; this is one of the reasons for which he tends to love intelligence tests. And what applies in the case of the mentally deficient applies also in the case of any other mental classification. The man who deals affectionately with a small group of children knows them as individuals, and feels things about them which it would be difficult to put into words; often it is what is peculiar to a child that such a man likes best. But the man who views children from a distance, through a mist of official reports, is impatient of this sort of thing. He wishes all children were exactly alike, since that would make his work easy, but he is compelled to admit classification by age, sex, nationality, and religion. The most enlightened also admit classification by intelligence tests. But even the most enlightened like everything cut and dried, and forget the quality of individual life which makes each human being different from every other. For this reason there is a danger lest education officials should encourage a uniformity towards which, in any case, the world is tending.

This is an administrative problem, and it has an administrative solution, namely, devolution. (If there were a world-government, it would no doubt exercise a certain degree of supervision over all education: it would forbid excessive teaching of local patriotism, and it might prohibit doctrines which it considered subversive. But in all other respects it would, no doubt, leave education to be organized locally. If it were inspired by a scientific spirit, it would also permit various experiments in new methods. The experimental spirit is, at present, foreign to most administrators, but if education were more scientific it would become much commoner. It is to the growth of the experimental spirit that we must look for the toleration of loopholes and exceptions in the scientific State. Without loopholes and exceptions, there will be little progress and insufficient diversity; but this, I think, may come to be believed by officials when they have all had a sound scientific education, not only in physics and chemistry, but also in biology.

(Individualism, although it is important not to forget its just claims, needs, in a densely populated industrial world, to be more controlled, even in individual psychology, than in former times. Those of us who have lived in large cities have all acquired ways of behaviour in crowds which are such as to prevent confusion: we keep to the right, move at the proper speed, and cross streets where we should. These are small and external matters, but

243

something of the same sort is required in more serious concerns. St. John the Baptist used to go about insufficiently clad, exclaiming "Repent ye: for the Kingdom of Heaven is at hand." If a man were to do this in London or New York, he would collect such a crowd that the traffic would be blocked, and the police would have to tell him that he must hire a hall before again uttering his sentiments. Very few men in an industrial society are independent units in their work; the vast majority belong to organizations, and have to carry out their portion of a collective undertaking. A sense of citizenship, of social co-operation, is therefore more necessary than it used to be; but it remains important that this should be secured without too great a diminution of individual judgement and individual initiative.

If a man's life is to be satisfactory, whether from his own point of view or from that of the world at large, it requires two kinds of harmony: an internal harmony of intelligence, emotion, and will, and an external harmony with the wills of others. In both these respects, existing education is defective. Internal harmony is prevented by the religious and moral teaching given in infancy and youth, which usually continues to govern the emotions but not the intelligence in later life, while the will is left vacillating, inclining to one side or the other according as emotion or intelligence has momentarily the upper hand. Such conflicts could be pre-

244

vented if the young were taught doctrines which adult intelligence can accept. This can be done in private schools on a small scale, but without the co-operation of the State it cannot be done on a sufficiently large scale to produce results having other than experimental importance.

(The matter of external harmony with the wills of others is more difficult, and not capable of a complete solution. Competition and co-operation are both natural human activities, and it is difficult to suppress competition completely without destroying individuality. But it is not individual and unorganized competition that does the harm in the modern world. Two men may compete for the same woman without harm to any one, provided their rivalry stops short of murder. The dangerous form of disharmony in the modern world is the organized form, between nations and between classes. So long as this form of disharmony persists, the world cannot enjoy the advantages which science and technical skill have made possible. The disharmony between nations is encouraged by education in the present day, and could be brought to an end by the introduction of internationalist propaganda in schools. This, however, is hardly possible without a previous victory of political internationalism. Education can consolidate political achievements, but is not likely to cause them so long as it is controlled by national States.

There have been times when competition in the

form of war was advantageous to the victors. Those times are past. It is obvious now, to every thinking person, that every nation would be happier if all armed forces everywhere were disbanded and all disputes between nations were settled by an international tribunal and all tariffs were abolished and all men could move freely from one country to another. Science has so altered our technique as to make the world one economic unit. But our political institutions and beliefs lag behind our technique, and each nation makes itself artificially poor by economic isolation. We invent labour-saving devices and are troubled by unemployment. When we cannot sell our products, we cut down wages, under the impression, apparently, that the less men earn the more they will spend. All these evils arise from one source, that, while our technique demands co-operation of the whole human race as a single producing and consuming unit, our passions and our political beliefs persist in demanding competition.

Our world is a mad world. Ever since 1914 it has ceased to be constructive, because men will not follow their intelligence in creating international co-operation, but persist in retaining the division of mankind into hostile groups. This collective failure to use the intelligence that men possess for purposes of self-preservation is due, in the main, to the insane and destructive impulses which lurk in the unconscious of those who have been unwisely handled in infancy, childhood, and adolescence. In spite of continually improving technique in production, we all grow poorer. In spite of being well aware of the horrors of the next war, we continue to cultivate in the young those sentiments which will make it inevitable. In spite of science, we react against the habit of considering problems rationally. In spite of increasing command over nature, most men feel more hopeless and impotent than they have felt since the Middle Ages. The source of all this does not lie in the external world, nor does it lie in the purely cognitive part of our nature, since we know more than men ever knew before. It lies in our passions; it lies in our emotional habits; it lies in the sentiments instilled in youth, and in the phobias created in infancy. (The cure for our problem is to make men sane, and to make men sane they must be educated sanely. At present the various factors we have been considering all tend towards social disaster. Religion encourages stupidity, and an insufficient sense of reality; sex education frequently produces nervous disorders, and where it fails to do so overtly, too often plants discords in the unconscious which make happiness in adult life impossible; nationalism as taught in schools implies that the most important duty of young men is homicide; class feeling promotes acquiescence in economic injustice; and competition promotes ruthlessness in the social struggle. Can it be wondered at that a world in which the forces of the

State are devoted to producing in the young insanity, stupidity, readiness for homicide, economic injustice, and ruthlessness—can it be wondered at, I say, that such a world is not a happy one? Is a man to be condemned as immoral and subversive because he wishes to substitute for these elements in the moral education of the present day intelligence, sanity, kindliness, and a sense of justice? The world has become so intolerably tense, so charged with hatred, so filled with misfortune and pain that men have lost the power of balanced judgement which is needed for emergence from the slough in which mankind is staggering. Our age is so painful that many of the best men have been seized with despair. But there is no rational ground for despair: the means of happiness for the human race exist, and it is only necessary that the human race should choose to use them.

INDEX

INDEX

GEORGE ALLEN & UNWIN LTD
London: 40 Museum Street, W.C.1
Cape Town: 73 St. George's Street
Sydney, N.S.W.: Wynyard Square
Auckland, N.Z.: 41 Albert Street
Toronto: 91 Wellington Street, West

Printed in the United Kingdom
by Lightning Source UK Ltd.
123041UK00001B/399/A

9 781406 733266